D0115506

ACCIDENTS

In North American Climbing 2016

Volume 11 | Number 1 | Issue 69

the **AMERICAN ALPINE club**

AMERICAN ALPINE CLUB
GOLDEN, COLORADO

ALPINE CLUB OF CANADA
CANMORE, ALBERTA

© 2016 The American Alpine Club

All rights reserved. No part of this publication may be reproduced or transmitted in any form or by any means, electronic or mechanical, including photocopying, recording, or any information and retrieval systems, without permission from the publisher.

ISBN: 978-1-933056-93-7
ISBN (e-book): 978-1-933056-94-4

Manufactured in the United States. Published by the American Alpine Club, 710 Tenth Street, Suite 100, Golden, CO, 80401, www.americanalpineclub.org.

Photos

Front Cover Suzan DeBruin and Travis Weil starting up the second pitch of Second Coming at Looking Glass, North Carolina. Photo by Karsten Delap.

Table of Contents A climber on the east ridge of Mt. Logan in the Yukon. Photo by Bryce Brown.

Back Cover Rescuers at work on Mt. Hood in Oregon. Photo courtesy of Portland Mountain Rescue

WARNING!

The activities described within *Accidents in North American Climbing* (ANAC)—including but not limited to: rock climbing, ice climbing, mountaineering, backcountry skiing, or any other outdoor activity—carry a significant risk of personal injury or death. The owners, staff, contributors, and volunteers that create this publication recommend that you DO NOT participate in these activities unless you are an expert, have sought or obtained qualified professional instruction or guidance, are knowledgeable about the risks involved, and are willing to assume personal responsibility for all the risks associated with these activities. ANAM and its publisher, the American Alpine Club, MAKE NO WARRANTIES, EXPRESSED OR IMPLIED, OF ANY KIND REGARDING THE CONTENTS OF THIS PUBLICATION, AND EXPRESSLY DISCLAIM ANY WARRANTY REGARDING THE ACCURACY OR RELIABILITY OF INFORMATION CONTAINED HEREIN. The American Alpine Club further disclaims any responsibility for injuries or death incurred by any person engaging in these activities. Use the information contained in this publication at your own risk, and do not depend on the information contained herein for personal safety or for determining whether to attempt any climb, route, or activity described herein. The examples/stories contained herein are anecdotal and/or informational only and not intended to represent advice, recommendations, or commentary on appropriate conduct, standards or choices that you, the reader, may make regarding your own activities.

Photo © www.kalice.fr

GRIGRI 2

Your very own personal belay assistant.

The GRIGRI 2 is the gold standard for assisted braking belay devices. Compact and lightweight, it works with single dynamic ropes from 8.9 to 11mm. Its unique design also provides excellent control while lowering. www.petzl.com

Access
the
inaccessible

ACCIDENTS IN NORTH AMERICAN CLIMBING

American Alpine Club

EDITOR EMERITUS
John E. (Jed) Williamson

EDITOR
Dougald MacDonald

ASSOCIATE EDITORS
Aram Attarian, Erik Rieger

REGIONAL EDITORS
Andy Anderson (UT); Aram Attarian (Southeast); Lindsay Auble & Lee Smith (CO); Marc Beverly & Erin Weber (NM); Stacia Glenn & Eddie Espinosa (WA); Sarah Koniewicz & Ryan Sommers (Midwest); Dara Miles (PA); R. Bryan Simon (WV); Eric Ratkowski (Shawangunks, NY); Michael Wejchert (NH)

DESIGN
Sarah Nicholson, David Boersma

ADDITIONAL THANKS
Ron Funderburke, Liberty Mountain, Leo Paik, Jim Pasterczyk, Joel Peach, Petzl, Michael Skaug, Robert Speik, Sterling, Jed Williamson, Keegan Young

Alpine Club of Canada

CHAIR, SAFETY COMMITTEE
Hai Pham
safety@alpineclubofcanada.ca

CANADIAN CONTENT EDITOR
Robert Chisnall
anam@alpineclubofcanada.ca

CONTENTS

Photo by Bryce Brown

PREFACE

The 69th Annual Edition
By Dougald MacDonald

Readers will notice two significant changes in this year's edition. The first is right on the cover: We've updated the name to *Accidents in North American Climbing* to reflect the evolving nature of modern technical climbing. Well over half the incidents covered in each year's edition now involve rock climbing instead of mountaineering. And the great majority of new climbers—the ones who will benefit most from our lessons—are primarily rock climbers. A flip through the pages will quickly show that we are firmly committed to covering mountaineering in this book. But we want to ensure that *all* climbers understand that *Accidents in North American Climbing* is a resource for them.

That's not all that's new. For the first time in this book's nearly 70-year history, we are publishing in full color. Our new Sharp End podcast, hosted by Ashley Saupe and based on the stories in these pages, is growing by leaps and bounds. (Find it at iTunes or Soundcloud.) Our corps of volunteer regional editors has expanded significantly, adding local expertise to our reporting. If you have a passion for climbing safety and an interest in journalistic coverage of climbing accidents, ask about joining our volunteer team at *accidents@americanalpineclub.org.*

In collaboration with the American Alpine Club's new education program, we are dedicated to fostering safer, smarter climbers. If you have suggestions or comments, write to me at *accidents@americanalpineclub.org.*

CONTRIBUTE

Submissions
Accidents in North American Climbing depends on detailed incident reports from injured climbers, their partners, search and rescue organizations, and park officials. First-person reports or analyses of climbing accidents or near misses are encouraged. Visit *publications.americanalpineclub.org/accidents_submission* to file a report online or email us at *accidents@americanalpineclub.org.*

Friends of Accidents
The following people and organizations have recently donated $100 or more specifically to support *Accidents.* Thank you! Make your own contribution at *americanalpineclub.org/donate.*

Charles Eiriksson
Michael Heathfield
Stephen Johnson
Liberty Mountain

Dougald MacDonald
Gary McElvany
Mountain Shop
William Oliver
Scott Petersen

Sierra Madre Search
& Rescue Team
Gary Treml
Jolene Unsoeld
Andrew Walker

BEAL
STINGER

UNICORE®
TECHNOLOGY
FOR YOUR
SECURITY

BEAL ATHLETE
JEWELL LUND
MERRIMAKER 5.11A, GREEN ADJECTIVE GULLY
LITTLE COTTONWOOD CANYON, UTAH

Liberty
Mountain

Distributed in North America by Liberty Mountain
For a dealer near you call 1-888.90.CLIMB
Photo: Nathan Smith - http://www.pullphotography.com

AAC RESCUE BENEFITS

Since 1948, the American Alpine Club has published *Accidents in North American Climbing* to increase climbers' knowledge and prevent climbing accidents. But prevention doesn't work every time. Whether you're close to home or climbing on a faraway expedition, the AAC's rescue benefits provide peace of mind in case something goes wrong.

Members of the American Alpine Club are automatically enrolled for $12,500 of rescue benefits: $7,500 in Global Rescue services worldwide (including the U.S.), plus $5,000 in Domestic Rescue benefits to reimburse members for out-of-pocket rescue expenses in the United States.

In 2015 alone, 30 American Alpine Club members were rescued around the globe.

COVERAGE

Global Rescue ($7,500)

This benefit covers you anywhere in the world for rescue and evacuation by or under the direction of Global Rescue personnel. If you're injured beyond the trailhead, no matter the elevation, we will come to your aid. Members who want more than $7,500 of coverage can upgrade at a 5% discount by visiting americanalpineclub.org/rescue. TO USE THIS BENEFIT: Call +1 (617) 459-4200 as soon as possible during an emergency.

Domestic Rescue ($5,000)

This benefit reimburses AAC members for out-of-pocket rescue costs in the United States. This benefit can be used in addition to the Global Rescue service. TO USE THIS BENEFIT: File a claim within 60 days of evacuation by calling (303) 384-0110 or emailing claims@americanalpineclub.org. We will send you a check.

Activities Covered

Climbing, hiking, backcountry skiing, mountain biking and more. If it's human-powered, on land, and you're rescued, you're covered as long as you're an active AAC member.

JOIN THE AAC

Only active members of the American Alpine Club may use these services. To join, visit www.americanalpineclub.org/join or call (303) 384-0110. You will gain access to $12,500 of rescue benefits as soon as you pay dues. As a member you also will be supporting the publication of this book, and you'll receive free copies of the latest *Accidents in North American Climbing* and *American Alpine Journal*, among many other benefits.

STERLING®

Evolution Aero 9.2 mm
in teal (56 g/M). CE 0120

Sterling is a certified
ISO 9001 company.

SECURITY

In an era of outsourcing, we've made a commitment to US-made quality. Every Sterling rope is designed, tested and produced under one roof in Biddeford, ME. This means reliable and better performing ropes for all conditions.

sterlingrope.com

Made in U.S.A.

with U.S. and Globally Sourced Material.

Know the Ropes

BELAYING

BY RON FUNDERBURKE

Climbers have been belaying for as long as they've been using ropes. We use some type of belay in almost every roped climbing context—it is the essential skill that unites all disciplines. It's interesting, therefore, to see how little agreement there is about the "best" belay techniques, how distracting our assertions about belaying tend to be, and how rigidly dogmatic we can be about a task that many understand so imperfectly.

This dogmatic approach persists even though using a rope to belay something valuable—whether a load of cargo on a ship or a climber on a cliff—has always been organized by three fundamental principles:

- There should be a brake hand on the rope at all times.
- Any time the brake hand slides along the rope, the rope should be in the brake position.
- The hands and limbs should be positioned according to their natural strength.

These are the principles that we should use to evaluate belaying, yet our discussion of "good" or "bad" belaying often revolves around a specific biomechanical sequence. It's time to abandon this way of talking and thinking about belaying. It's misleading, reductive, and provokes more arguments that it solves.

Meanwhile, a cursory perusal of any edition of *Accidents* reveals there are severe consequences for imprecise understanding of belaying. In recent years, 5 to 10 percent of all incidents reported have involved inadequate belays.

This edition of Know the Ropes will equip readers with language and principles that unify all belay contexts. Additionally, for those who are new to belaying, those who want to learn to belay in different contexts, or those who aren't sure about their current technique, this article will provide some suggestions for how to do so in a fundamentally sound way. These are the same fundamentals that are being promoted through the American Alpine Club's new Universal Belay Standard. (*See sidebar on page 20.*)

> ### THREE FUNDAMENTALS
> • Keep your brake hand on the rope
> • Slide your hands only when the rope is in the braking position
> • Position your hands according to your natural strength

THE ORIGINS OF BELAYING PRINCIPLES

The earliest belayers used the most primitive technique: The belayer held the rope tightly and did not let go under any circumstance. Belayers had to be very strong, and the rope had to be kept very tight. And the brake hand had to be on the rope at all times. Even the strongest belayers and the lightest climbers wouldn't stand a chance without this fundamental principle.

In the early days of rock climbing, belayers simply held on tight, with no friction or mechanical advantage to assist them.

A friction belay around a horn can be a quick way to secure the second climber on some routes. *Ron Funderburke*

The addition of friction to the belay system allowed smaller belayers to secure bigger climbers. Wrapping the rope around features in mountain terrain or the belayer's body provided enough friction to hold larger loads.

Friction also introduced two new realities to belaying. First, friction could be increased and decreased, creating a "belay cycle." Increased friction is valuable when holding a load; decreased friction is valuable when trying to move rope through the system.

The second new reality was that friction allowed the belayer to relax a little. In the more primitive form of belaying, without friction, the belayer's hand-over-hand technique maintained a constant grip on the rope. By contrast, a belay system with friction allows the belayer to relax his or her grip at some points in the cycle, which, naturally, deprioritizes vigilance.

These changes led to the second fundamental principle of belaying: Since every belay cycle has a point of high friction, it makes sense to spend as much time in that position as possible. Therefore, whenever the brake hand slides along the rope, the rope should be in the brake position. If a climber falls while the brake hand is sliding on the rope, it obviously will be easier and quicker to arrest the fall if the rope is already in the brake position.

Since the addition of friction to the system, every major evolution in belaying has involved some sort of technology. First came the carabiner, which not only allowed belayers to augment their friction belays but also invited the use of hitches, tied to carabiners, as belay tools. The most effective of these was the Munter hitch.

The Munter hitch offered a braking position that was the same as the pulling position, so the belay cycle was easy to teach and learn. It soon became the predominant belay technique in all disciplines. (Before the advent of reliable protection, dynamic belays, and nylon ropes, belaying was primarily the duty of the leader. A second might belay the leader, but the leader was not expected to fall, nor was it widely expected that a leader fall could be caught.) The Munter hitch, belaying a second from above, conforms naturally to the third fundamental principle of belaying: It positions the hands, limbs, and body according to their natural strength. It keeps the belay comfortable and strong throughout the belay cycle, and while taking rope in, catching falls, holding weight, and lowering.

THE MODERN ERA

An era ago, these fundamental principles were not really in dispute. They applied to body belays (hip belays, butt belays, shoulder belays, boot-axe belays, etc.), terrain belays (belays over horns, boulders, and ridgelines), and belays on carabiners (Munter hitch). However, by the Second World War, climbers began to use nylon ropes and other equipment that could handle the forces of leader falls. Moreover, climbing clubs, schools, and enthusiasts began to experiment with redirecting the climbing rope through a top anchor, so that belaying on the ground, for both the leader and follower, became much more common. Pushing the limits of difficulty also became more common—leading to more falling.

Belayers around the world also began to experiment with new belay tools that redirected the braking position 180 degrees—the most common early example was the Sticht plate, but the same principle applies to today's tube-style devices. Instead of the brake strand of rope running in the same direction as the loaded strand (the climb-

A direct belay off an anchor with a Munter hitch.

er's strand), the belayer had to hold the brake strand in the opposite direction.

For many years, instructors and textbooks explained how to use these new manual belay devices (MBDs) by defaulting to the hand and body positions that had become entrenched from the use of the Munter hitch and the hip belay. The most common of these was the hand-up (supinated) brake-hand position on the rope.

The stronger, more comfortable technique with MBDs is a hand-down (pronated) position with the brake hand, and newer texts and instructors often adopted this technique, in order to connect the new technology with the fundamental principles of belay. But the resulting cacophony—with belay instruction varying wildly—gave students and climbers the impression that belaying did not have any governing principles.

We climbers have our sectarian instincts, and climbers today are as likely to argue the relative merits of various belay techniques as they are to argue about the merits of sport climbing and trad climbing, alpine style and expedition style. The goal of this article is to redirect all belayers' attention to two indisputable truths:

- Belaying happens in many, many different contexts.
- Belaying in *every* context is most effective when it is based on the three fundamental principles, which long preceded any arguments we are currently having.

| Pull in Slack | Slide Brake Hand Back | Brake if Necessary |

THE CONTEXTS OF BELAYING

Even though we generally learn to belay in a fairly simple context (top-roping), belaying is much more diverse than what happens in an Intro to Climbing class. The most appropriate belay techniques can vary widely depending on the setting (gym, multi-pitch crag, alpine climb, etc.) and whether the climber is leading or following. Most generally, belaying happens in three different ways, using different techniques and tools for each: friction belays, counterweight belays, and direct belays.

FRICTION BELAYS

In a friction belay, the rope runs directly between the belayer and climber, and there might not be any anchor. The potential holding power of the belay is relative to the amount of friction one can generate, the strength of the belayer's grip, and the resilience of the object providing friction.

Friction belays are most common in mountaineering (though there are other contexts where they provide efficient and prudent options). In the mountains, there usually are long stretches of terrain where a full anchor is not necessary and building and deconstructing anchors might dangerously delay the climbers.

Most commonly, the belayer will select a feature of the terrain to belay or use his or her body to create friction. The belay stance must replace the security that an anchor might have provided, whether by bracing one's feet, belaying over the top of a ridgeline, or another method. Any terrain features used to provide friction or a stance must be carefully inspected to ensure they are solid and won't create a rockfall hazard.

COUNTERWEIGHT BELAYS

Whether climbing single-pitch routes or belaying the leader on a multi-pitch climb, these are the most commonly used belay techniques. The climbing rope is redirected through a top anchor or a leader's top piece of protection, and the belayer provides a counterweight, coupled with effective belay technique and tools, to hold or lower the climber or catch a fall.

Even though there are plenty of exceptions, the vast majority of American climbing happens in a single-pitch setting, on a climb that is less than 30 meters tall. The belayers and climbers generally are comparably sized, and the belayer is comfortably situated on the ground. Belaying this way provides a more social atmosphere, allowing for banter, camaraderie, and coaching. That's why climbing gyms, climbing programs, and most casual outings gravitate toward this belay context.

However, the ease and comfort of single-pitch counterweight belays do not liberate the belayer from serious responsibilities. Thankfully, there are several different biomechanical sequences for belaying a top-rope that fall under the halo of the three fundamental principles. Each of the three techniques outlined below comes with a set of pros and cons that makes it the preferred methods of certain groups of climbers, instructors, and programs.

PBUS

The top-roping belay technique commonly known as PBUS resonates with climbing instructors and mentors because it emphasizes the fundamental principles so

| Pull | Brake | Under | Slide |

distinctly. The hand transition is securely in the braking position, and it's hard to imagine the belayer losing control if the climber were to fall while the hand was sliding. Plus, the ergonomics of the technique keep the wrist and grip pronated.

PBUS is most effective when a top-roper is moving slowly and hanging frequently. When the climber moves quickly and proficiently, a strict adherence to this technique often causes the belay setup to collapse, which could allow the belay carabiner to cross-load. It's also harder to move slack quickly enough to keep up with a proficient climber.

HAND OVER HAND

If the belayer alternates brake hands, he or she is able to move slack through the belay cycle more quickly than with PBUS. As long as the brake hands are alternating in the braking position, this technique abides by the fundamental principles of belay, and it is a preferred technique for experienced belayers and for top-ropers who move quickly.

Many instructors and mentors dislike this technique because it allows the belayer to keep "a" brake hand on at all times, instead of keeping "the" brake hand on at all times. As a result, this technique is usually relegated to more experienced teams.

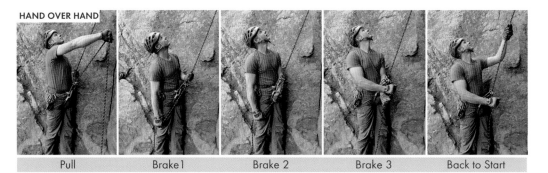

| Pull | Brake 1 | Brake 2 | Brake 3 | Back to Start |

SHUFFLE

The shuffle technique is most applicable when using an assisted-braking device (ABD) to belay, but it can be used with manual devices by a very experienced be-layer. It requires the belayer to have a refined sense of how to grip the rope with varying degrees of intensity, all without relinquishing the readiness to brake. A loosely gripped brake hand can shuffle along the brake strand, up or down, without letting go. A tightly gripped brake hand can be used to catch falls.

Many belayers find this technique unsettling because they are attached to the idea that a relentlessly strong grip on the brake strand is symbolic of the belayer's commitment. With a proficient belayer, however, the shuffle technique is not only fundamentally sound, it also can be a smooth and reliable way to belay, especially with an ABD.

BELAYING A LEADER

Lead belaying involves the same fundamental counterweight arrangements

| Pull | Brake | Shuffle |

as top-rope belays, but the dynamics involved in a lead fall greatly augment the forces a belayer must contend with. The loads can be severe and startling. Moreover, there is much more to effective lead belaying than simply paying out slack and catching occasional falls. The interplay of slack and tension requires quick and seamless adaptation, practiced and undistracted fine motor skills, and a situational awareness that is hard to achieve if one has never done any leading oneself. Lead belayers must master the following skills:

- Setup and preparation
- Correct use of the chosen belay device
- Compensating for unnecessary slack
- Catching falls

Unfortunately, lead belayers may only learn a portion of these skills before they are asked to perform all of them on a belay. It's easy to imagine how a rudimentary skill set can result in frustration, accidents, or even fatalities.

SETUP AND PREPARATION

A lead belayer needs to determine the likely fall line for a climber who has clipped the first piece of protection. Standing directly beneath the first piece and then taking one step out of the fall line (roughly 10 degrees) will usually keep a falling leader from landing directly on the belayer's head, while still keeping the belayer in position to give an effective belay.

Once the lead belayer decides where he or she wants to stand, the rope should be stacked neatly on the brake-hand side, right next to the belayer's stance. A knot in the belayer's end of the rope (or tying in) closes the system.

USING THE BELAY DEVICE

Lead belayers will have to learn some fine motor skills to offer an effective lead belay, especially with an ABD. It takes practice.

Most of the time, the leader keeps his or her brake hand wrapped entirely around the rope, as with any other belay. The lead belayer pays out arm lengths of slack as the leader moves, and then slides the brake hand down the rope with the rope in the brake position. The mechanics are mostly identical, whether the belayer is using an MBD (such as an ATC or other tube-style device) or an ABD.

But when the leader moves quickly or pulls a lot of slack to clip protection, the belayer will have to feed slack fast, without releasing the brake hand. This is easily learned with an MBD, using a form of the shuffle technique. But with ABD devices such as the Grigri, a specific technique for each device must be learned and practiced. Follow the manufacturer's instructions and warnings. (Most have produced instructional online videos explaining the appropriate technique.) No matter which device you use, keep the fundamental principles of belaying in mind. Most importantly, your brake hand must stay on the rope as you feed slack.

COMPENSATING

Lead belaying also involves a subtle exchange of giving and taking rope called compensating. When a leader makes a long clip, there is a moment where the rope is

BELAYING A HEAVIER CLIMBER

When the climber and the belayer are not comparably sized, the physics of the counterweight can have significant consequences. It won't matter terribly if the belayer is much heavier than the climber. But when the climber is much heavier than the belayer—especially when a climber is leading—an effective counterweight will be difficult to achieve.

In general, the belayer's mass should be at least 60 percent of the climber's mass. For example, if the climber weighs 185 pounds, the belayer should weigh at least 111 pounds (185 X 0.6 = 111).

If the weight discrepancy exceeds these margins, the belayer will require an anchor or ballast (such as backpacks or another person) in order to serve as an effective counterweight. The belayer should be connected to the ballast with no slack in the tether, and the system should run in a straight line from the ground anchor, through the belayer, and toward the upper anchor or climber (*see photo*).

actually clipped above the leader's head, and he or she is effectively on a short top-rope. As a result the belayer needs to make a seamless transition between giving slack, taking in slack, and giving slack again. The most extreme version of compensating happens when the leader downclimbs from a clip to a rest and then reascends to the high point.

CATCHING FALLS

The most important part of catching a fall is stopping a leader from hitting the ground or a ledge—or abruptly slamming into the wall. On overhanging climbs, a leader is less likely to impact objects, so longer falls are acceptable. But on vertical or low-angled climbs, the same length of fall could easily cause the leader to impact features along the fall line.

The lead belayer must be constantly prepared to mitigate the fall consequence as much as he or she can, and a key part of this is maintaining the appropriate amount of slack and movement in the system. While belaying a leader on an overhang, the belayer might feel free to let the momentum of the counterweight lift him off the ground. This is the coveted "soft catch" that so many leaders seem to think is essential.

But when a fall is more consequential—when it might result in ledge impact or a ground fall—an astute belayer may "fight" the fall, sometimes even taking in slack and bracing to increase the counterweight effect.

It takes time and effort to learn this distinction, because every climb is a little different. One of the most important ways to learn lead belaying is to lead climb.

An experienced leader will better understand the issues facing other lead climbers and will know what it feels like to have a belayer do his or her job perfectly.

DIRECT BELAYS

Direct belays connect the belay system directly to an anchor. As a result, the anchor must be fundamentally sound. That is to say, it has redundant construction, distributes loads intelligently to all the components, limits potential shock-loading if a single component were to fail, and is adequately strong. The anchor must easily sustain all the potential loads applied to it, plus a healthy margin of error. Its integrity should not be in question.

Direct belays are the most prudent way to belay a second from the top of a rock or ice pitch where falls are likely and consequential. (That would include all fifth-class rock terrain and almost every ice climb at any grade.) They do not trap the belayer in a counterweight arrangement, allowing the belayer to manage the rope and multitask. Because the belayer is attached to the anchor separately, the belayer can affect assistance techniques to help a climber move up if needed. Direct belays

(Top) When a leader falls on overhanging terrain, the belayer can often "ride" the fall to give a "soft catch" and prevent the leader from being pulled hard into the wall. **(Bottom)** By contrast, on vertical or low-angled climbs, or anytime the leader might impact a ledge or other obstacle, it's often better for the belayer to brace and "fight" the fall to minimize the fall distance. *Ted Distel*

also put less force on an anchor than counterweight belays do (which shouldn't matter, really, because the anchor should be bombproof). Lastly, they are particularly advantageous when belaying more than one person simultaneously.

Whether the belayer is using a Munter hitch, an MBD, or an ABD in a direct belay, the fundamentals apply: The brake hand is always on the rope, hand transitions occur in the braking position, and the limbs are positioned in ways that are comfortable and sustainable. Direct belays should confer all of the climber's weight to the anchor, so it is easy to imagine a few different hand positions that

THE UNIVERSAL BELAY STANDARD

In the United States, every climbing gym, school program, and climbing instructor teaches some form of belaying. They also test belayers to ensure they meet a minimum standard. However, the standards to which they teach and test are not always consistent. With no national standard to distinguish fundamentally sound variations in belay technique from dangerous variations, all variations tend to be tolerated—and that leads to accidents.

The American Alpine Club (AAC) has begun working with institutions around the country to adopt a national standard and educate climbers on the fundamental principles that should govern all belaying—the same principles outlined in this article. Soon it will be possible to take the AAC Universal Belay Standard course at your local gym, club, school, or course provider. You will receive a Universal Belay Certificate that will give you and your partners confidence in your ability to belay safely.

Many helpful resources, including video demonstrations of the Universal Belay Standard in practice, can be found at the AAC website, along with a list of gyms and climbing schools that teach fundamentally sound belaying: *americanalpineclub. org/education.*

take advantage of the belayer's natural strength.

Lowering is a completely different story with direct belays. As articles in *Accidents* will attest, lowering will usually require the belayer to disable or reduce a device's autoblocking or braking function. As a result, the belayer should redirect the rope through the anchor and use a friction hitch or backup belay whenever he or she is lowering from a directl belay. (*See page 63 for a photo illustration of one backup method.*)

FINAL THOUGHTS

As we can see, there are so many variables to belaying that it can be counterproductive to say there is only one "right" technique. The appropriate belay method for each pitch depends on the terrain, the style and difficulty of climbing, the relative experience and weight of the climber and belayer, and the tools available. The "right" technique is the one that's appropriate for each context, as long as it adheres to the fundamental principles of keeping your brake hand on the rope, sliding your hand only when the rope is in the braking position, and positioning your hands and body according to their natural strength.

Ron Funderburke, an AMGA-certified Rock Guide, is the AAC's Education Director and author of half a dozen climbing instruction books.

The Grand Teton, high point of the Teton Range, from the Climbers' Ranch. *Brad Schwarm*

Danger Zones

THE GRAND TETON

BY JOEL PEACH

When Glenn Exum made the first ascent of the upper south ridge of the Grand Teton in 1931, he did so ropeless and wearing football cleats two sizes too large. The 18-year-old aspiring mountain guide negotiated an exposed traverse by leaping from the end of Wall Street ledge to gain the south ridge, which he followed to the summit.

Five years later, Jack Durrance and Kenneth Henderson climbed the lower section of the southern ridge and joined Exum's route to the top. The upper Exum Ridge and the original Owen-Spalding Route—first climbed in 1898—on the peak's west face are still the most popular ways to summit the Grand Teton during the busy summer season.

The carefree style of Exum's ascent notwithstanding, an ascent of the Grand by any route is a serious undertaking. The standard route through Garnet Canyon from the Lupine Meadows Trailhead gains about 7,000 feet, including about 1,700 feet of third- to fifth-class terrain, by the time one stands at the summit marker. Navigation can be inobvious, snow travel often presents hazards on the ways up and down, and variable mountain weather presents risks of lightning, ice-glazed rock, and hypothermia.

Underestimating the hazards of these routes has resulted in numerous serious (and in many cases avoidable) injuries, rescues, and deaths. While one may deem the number of incidents commensurate with the popularity of the climbs, it's worth noting that one in four of the Exum and Owen-Spalding incidents reported in *Accidents* resulted in a fatality. The stakes can be high on the Grand Teton. By analyzing the incidents reported in *Accidents*, we hope to offer guidance to future parties, so they can enjoy the alpine majesty of a Grand Teton climb while mitigating its perils.

METHODOLOGY

We searched *Accidents'* online database (*publications.americanalpineclub.org*) for all incidents related to the Grand Teton with a stated objective of either the Exum Ridge or Owen-Spalding Route (which is also the main descent route for all climbs of the Grand).

Most climbers approach and descend these routes via Garnet Canyon, so we included incidents taking place there, provided climbers were on their way to or from a route above the Lower Saddle, regardless of objective. However, we excluded climbs on the canyon walls or neighboring peaks.

Our search returned 74 incident reports from 1950 through 2014, involving 78 parties. Most took place during the peak summer season from June to August. The incidents were roughly split between those taking place on ascent and descent–despite the conventional wisdom that "most" mountaineering accidents happen during the descent.

It's important to note that our data includes only the incidents reported in the pages of *Accidents in North American Climbing*. These reports typically cover the most significant technical climbing accidents on the Grand Teton every year, but other accidents and rescues–some that involve Grand Teton National Park rangers and others that don't–are not recorded in these pages. Rangers and other Teton experts reviewed our conclusions to ensure they were consistent with the complete accident record.

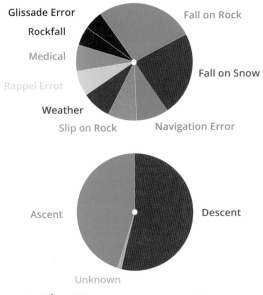

Accident Types. Design: MichaelSkaug.com

FALLS ON SNOW

Considering that 85 percent of the Grand Teton incidents took place during the summer, it might surprise climbers to learn the single most frequent contributing factor was a fall on snow. Overwhelmingly occurring during descents, these incidents were clustered among three main zones: at the upper end of the Garnet Canyon approach trail, around the Lower Saddle headwall, and between the Lower Saddle and Upper Saddle.

At the upper end of Garnet Canyon, the elevation is around 10,000 feet and the mountain retains snow for much of the year. Several of the reports from this zone described incidents involving moats (deep, crevasse-like slots found where snow-fields meet rock walls and boulders or where meltwater has carved

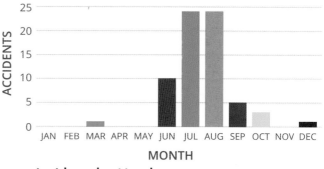

Accidents by Month. Design: MichaelSkaug.com

channels under the snow). In 1984, a climber fell on snow and was unperturbed enough to smile and wave at another climber as he slid past her, then he shot off a lip of snow into a moat and drowned. In 2013, a climber failed to follow a guide's instructions to wait for a rope before moving onto a snowfield; he too perished in a moat.

Higher up, just below the Lower Saddle, a snowfield whose bottom abuts the Middle Teton Glacier invites glissading during the descent. In three recorded instances, the climbers who initiated a glissade were unable to self-arrest. One climber in 1985 had been practicing ice axe techniques when a loss of control resulted in a lethal self-inflicted axe wound. In some cases the climbers who slipped in this area were either not carrying an ice axe or had left it strapped to their pack. In one case a guided, roped team was unable to prevent everyone from sliding several hundred meters, even though the guides were properly positioned and the climber who slipped attempted to arrest the fall.

Higher on the mountain, between the Lower Saddle and Upper Saddle, there are often snow patches and snow-filled gullies that can turn otherwise minor missteps into catastrophic events. The majority of the reported incidents occurring in this zone were fatal, owing to the exposure. Most parties were not carrying the proper gear to self-arrest, and those that did were often still injured.

RECOMMENDATIONS

Although the roped climbing on the Grand is mostly on rock, part of the appeal—and danger—of the mountain is that it requires a full range of alpine climbing skills. Snow conditions vary significantly from month to month and year to year—climbers should always inquire with rangers or local guide services to see whether an ice axe and/or crampons will be recommended for a given route. The Jenny Lake rangers' blog (*tetonclimbing.blogspot.com*) is a good source of condition reports during the climbing season.

If snow climbing is required, it's essential to know how to climb and descend steep snow and to self-arrest. The 2014 edition of *Accidents* included a feature article on snow travel (available at *publications.americanalpineclub.org*), and professional instruction in these techniques is widely available.

Variability of snow conditions during the day also should be considered. Many of the incidents reported in *Accidents* involved climbers who were lured onto firm or icy snow, fell or lost control of a glissade, and were unable to self-arrest. Others ventured onto sun-softened snow that was too slippery for kicking steps or that

Steep snow must be climbed and descended near the Lower Saddle in early season. **(Inset)** A moat along one side of this snowfield. In June 2013 a climber slid into a moat here and died. *David Bowers*

concealed harder, icier snow underneath. Wet snow also may ball up in crampons, rendering them useless. Late-summer snow can be particularly firm, as one incident analysis suggested: "The snowfields late in August are extremely hard and the use of crampons is almost a necessity when traveling any distance on them." However, climbers in late season often may be able to hike or scramble around patches of snow more easily. Always consider mitigating snow-travel risks with a belay if unexpectedly slippery terrain is encountered while descending.

George Montopoli, a veteran Grand Teton ranger and accident researcher, said his extensive database of Teton Range accidents shows the number of snow-travel accidents has declined in recent years, relative to other causes such as climbing falls, lightning, and rockfall. He suggested this was because of reduced snowfall and quicker melting in many recent summers. "We simply do not see the snow and other climatic conditions now that were present in the '70s and '80s," Montopoli said. Nonetheless, nearly every recent edition of *Accidents*, including this one, has reported falls on snow on or near the Grand.

FALLS ON ROCK

A quarter of the incidents surveyed involved a fall on rock, and the incidence of rock climbing falls has increased as a percentage of all accidents in recent years. These accidents almost always involved multiple contributing factors, the most common of which were solo/unroped travel and weather.

The modest technical difficulty of the Upper Exum Ridge and Owen-Spalding Route invite unroped climbing. Among climbers making their way alone or in teams without ropes, the accident reports show a variety of experience levels, ranging from a person in hiking boots who had only climbed in a gym twice before setting out to a veteran guide who fell to his death while soloing the Lower Exum. Different events precipitated the falls (broken holds, rockfall, wind gusts, etc.), but the decision to travel unroped and/or alone nearly always greatly amplified the consequences.

It's interesting to note that only two of the cases reported in *Accidents* involved a fall where a climber's protection pulled or failed. There were, however, cases where placing better and/or additional protection may have reduced the severity of falls. In one such case, a guide took a fatal 130-foot roped fall. (His client's life was most likely saved by a single nut placed at the belay.) In another incident, an off-route climber struck a ledge after taking a fall from a run-out position. In yet another, a seconding climber was injured in an unintended pendulum after slipping.

RECOMMENDATIONS

Regardless of ability, any decision to climb unroped or place minimal protection should give due consideration to objective hazards, including rockfall, dropped gear, icy or wet rock, loose holds, and other factors. An incident analysis from last year noted, "If this climber had been with a partner and roped up, with protection in place, his fall may have been minimal."

On more technical terrain, climbers should belay and place solid gear that is adequate to protect both the leader and those following. Experienced climbers may consider simul-climbing with some intermediate pro as an alternative to unroped travel on portions of the Upper Exum Ridge, giving some measure of protection against unexpected events. However, keep in mind that any fall while simul-climbing may involve both climbers, not just the leader.

WEATHER

The entire Owen-Spalding and Exum routes are above treeline, and exposure to poor weather continues until one is well down the trail into Garnet Canyon. Midday storms are common during the climbing season and bring with them the danger of lightning, high winds, hail, and snow. Snowstorms occurred during reported incidents on June 11, July 26, July 28, August 31, and September 12—covering nearly all of the summer season.

When the weather turned sour, many climbers in our reports made mistakes while attempting to beat storms to the summit or retreat away from them. Storms also increase the difficulty of the routes themselves. In 1999, a properly equipped leader fell from the Friction Pitch (the 5.4 crux of the Upper Exum) after a storm made the route icy and a wind gust blew him back.

Be prepared for weather to change the nature of the entire climb. An accident analysis in 1962 cautioned, "Nearly all storms in the Tetons leave the rock either ice-covered or wet and change most grade 3 climbs to grade 5 or 6, and also increase the amount of rockfall." Snow or icy rock may linger in shadowed areas of the routes long after a summer storm has passed.

Lightning is a particular hazard on the exposed upper mountain. Climbers have been struck by lightning bolts or ground currents on the Upper Exum, at Wall Street, and in the Owen Chimney on the Owen-Spalding Route. In an incident on July 26, 2003, a single lightning bolt appears to have sent electricity the entire length of the Exum Ridge, injuring several climbers, one fatally. The analysis of the 2003 accident noted that the party size was large (13 people), and combined with a late start and poor position on the mountain (arriving at Wall Street at 11 a.m.), this made it nearly impossible to safely retreat.

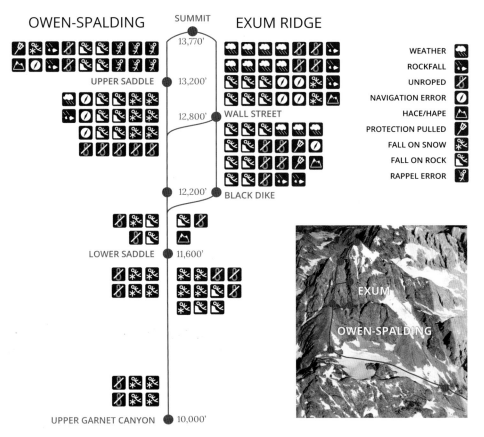

Accident Types by Location

Google Earth Image USDA Farm Service Agency Image © 2016 DigitalGlobe. Design: MichaelSkaug.com

RECOMMENDATIONS

In all but one of the reported lightning strikes, the parties were hit after noon. The earliest strike recorded in our reports was at 11:30 a.m. in August 1999. Descending from the upper mountain before noon greatly increases one's chances of avoiding lightning. However, an early start is not a guarantee of avoiding storm danger. Cold fronts passing through the area can add lift and instability to the atmosphere and, when coupled with existing moisture, may produce storms any time of day or night. Under certain conditions, monsoon moisture originating in Mexico can make its way to Wyoming, carrying greater cloud density and storm-producing humidity.

Mountain forecasts get stale quickly. Check local forecasts frequently and inquire with the Jenny Lake rangers about expected weather conditions as close as possible to your climb. In several incidents reported in these pages, park rangers had specifically cautioned climbers against ascents or certain routes due to conditions or weather.

Stay aware once you're on the route and be willing to change your plans. Early cloud build-up in Idaho, to the west of the mountain, is often a sign of impending storms. If you can hear thunder or see lightning flashes, you're close enough to be struck by lightning and should turn around. The book *Reading Weather*, by Tetons-based forecaster Jim Woodmencey, is an excellent introduction to meteorology and field forecasting.

ROUTEFINDING

One in ten incidents reported in *Accidents* involved a problem staying on route, either on the way up the mountain or during the descent. Getting off-route often means encountering more challenging terrain, with an increased risk of falling. Poorer quality rock also may be encountered off the main routes. Finally, losing the route leads to delays and potential stranding, greatly increasing the risk of weather-related trouble.

Ice axe blasted by lightning on the Grand Teton. *Jeff Witt*

RECOMMENDATIONS

Before you leave home, take advantage of guidebooks and online trip reports to familiarize yourself with the intended route. Photocopy descriptions of routes and the planned descent to carry with you. (Consider carrying descriptions of alternate routes in case your planned climb is crowded or you get off-route.) Once you arrive at the park, stop by the Jenny Lake Ranger Station to inquire about current conditions and route-finding advice.

Study the route ahead from your highest camp. During the climb, make a point of pausing as soon as it's light to note key landmarks of the route and descent. Be willing to retreat and know the options for doing so. However, there are few efficient options for retreat from the Upper Exum. Once high on the upper ridge, the best way off is to continue to the summit and descend the Owen-Spalding.

FINAL NOTES

A handful of reported incidents involved large parties, ranging up to 13 climbers. The analyses mentioned that larger parties can make it difficult to manage ascents safely—and may cause additional problems in a retreat.

A few instances of high-altitude illness have been reported, including high-altitude pulmonary edema (HAPE) or high-altitude cerebral edema (HACE). The risk of altitude illnesses increases above 8,000 feet, and the Grand rises to 13,776 feet. Give yourself time to acclimatize, especially if coming from lower elevations. Familiarize yourself with altitude illnesses' signs and symptoms, and descend if anyone in the partner is stricken.

In summary, those aiming to climb the Grand must have the equipment and skills to complete a varied alpine climb and deal with rapidly changing conditions. The huge elevation gain and miles of hiking, carrying heavy packs laden with camping and climbing gear, require climbers to be in excellent physical shape. Those who approach the Grand with the requisite information, expertise, physical conditioning, and equipment stand the best chance of enjoying this great mountain safely.

Thanks to Rich Baerwald, Chris Bellino, David Bowers, Bob Irvine, George Montopoli, Nat Patridge, Jed Williamson, and Jim Woodmencey for providing information and feedback for this article.

A climber crosses the Jago River near the scene of an accident in 2015. *Joe Stock | Stock Alpine*

ALASKA

RIVER CROSSING | Fatigue
Brooks Range, Arctic National Wildlife Refuge

Four friends—Dave, Edward, Greg, and Jill—planned to attempt Mt. Itso (8,975 feet) in the Brooks Range. The group flew to the upper Jago River landing site and crossed the river without incident. After five days of strenuous effort, via two different sides of the mountain, the group turned around on June 18, about 800 feet below the summit, in poor weather.

The retreat was exhausting, part of it spent post-holing to their thighs in soft late-afternoon snow along a creek described by Greg as "much swollen in volume due to precipitation and the time of day." After a 16-hour day they reached camp, soaked and exhausted.

They slept in late on the 19th and began hiking around noon toward the Jago River Valley, from which they planned to call for a flight out from the more accessible lower Jago River landing zone. In his account of the day, Greg noted that, "The middle fork of Trident Creek had been a pretty easy crossing two days ago, but was now quite the raging stream. We crossed it OK without ropes, but Dave and I talked to each other afterward, noticing that Edward seemed rather tentative and shaky as he made his way across."

After the crossing, Edward led the way most of the day. At the final talus slope, Greg came upon Edward sprawled on his back on a large, flat rock. Greg asked if he was OK. Edward replied, "barely," and explained that a rock had given way and he'd fallen. Greg reported that he seemed fine after a few minutes. The group examined his head for injuries and carried his pack across a few more yards of talus.

Dave told Greg he wanted to get the Jago River crossing done that evening, "so we'd have it over with." Edward concurred. Jill and Greg didn't object, although Greg mentioned that river levels were lower in the mornings.

At about 6 p.m., Edward spotted an 80-foot-wide, rapid-free stretch of river that looked promising. According to Greg, "We all agreed, either verbally or by lack of dissent, that this place seemed like our best bet."

They tied a 100-foot rope and 50-foot rope together with a double fisherman's knot. Greg put on his harness, tied into the end of the 50-foot rope, and set off. He reported, "There had been talk of the followers using a prusik knot, which would secure them to the rope, but the double fisherman's knot in the middle made that impossible. So the idea was to use a carabiner on a sling instead, which would pass over the knot but not connect the person to the rope firmly."

Using an ice axe for support, Greg successfully crossed the river, but the current forced him downstream with each step. The deepest part was about 2.5 feet, and he was forced to crouch to keep his stance, so the water was nearly to his waist. When he reached the other side he moved upstream to secure the rope directly across the river from his partners. Greg placed a sling around a rock, connected his harness to the sling so he could use his body weight to keep it in place, then attached the rope to his belay device.

Edward was ready to go first and clipped in to the main rope with a carabiner on a sling. He set off at about 6:15 p.m. He buckled the chest and waist straps on his frame pack for more load stability. His sleeping bag was attached to the outside bottom of his pack. Also using his ice axe for stability, Edward took a more direct route than Greg had, as he was forced to follow the taut rope. When he reached the deepest point, about two-thirds of the way across, he stopped and began to struggle. Edward was in almost waist-deep, and most of his pack and the sleeping bag were soaked.

Greg remembered, "After 30 seconds we were concerned for Edward. He was still upright but did not seem to be able to stabilize himself, and he was clearly in trouble. I was powerless to do anything and just sat there watching him, hoping he would somehow start making progress. I don't know if giving him some slack would have helped, but it didn't occur to me—unconsciously, I may have thought that a taut and stable rope would be the best solid anchor for him.... He made no attempt to unbuckle his pack, and it may have been dragging him down.

"The next thing I recall is seeing Dave, on the opposite bank, walk over to his big rock anchor and undo the coils holding the rope in place. I instantly grasped that his idea was that Edward would then be caught in the flow, and my anchor would then pendulum him over to my side of the river, where he would come ashore. Freed up, he could also perhaps ditch his pack or swim ashore.

"My recollection is that when the rope went loose, Edward suddenly went from his semi-upright stance to face-down in the water, under his pack, and started floating downstream like a log. He stopped briefly when I felt his weight on the rope in my belay device, and I held him for a second. But then the rope went suddenly slack, and I knew immediately that his sling carabiner had gone off the end of the rope. Under the weight of his pack, he was now sailing down the river in the current. I was shocked most by his lack of motion—he was not swimming, thrashing, or moving at all."

Dave ran along his side of the river and got downstream from Edward, swam out to him, and managed to pull his body to shore almost a mile below the crossing site. Edward had been in the water approximately 10 minutes. Dave and Jill began CPR immediately and took turns trying to save Edward's life for two hours, until 8:30 p.m. Greg used a satellite phone to call pilot Kirk Sweetsir, who notified county authorities, who then arranged for a helicopter.

ANALYSIS

Several factors contributed to this tragedy:

Group fatigue and possible injury during Edward's talus fall. There were indications before the river crossing that Edward was not functioning either physically or mentally at his optimum. During the crossing, he moved very slowly, lengthening his exposure to the cold water and possible hypothermia.

Lack of preparation for rigorous Alaskan river crossings. While the group had experience as climbers and mountaineers, they didn't know or use the best river crossing techniques.

Desire by the group to "get the crossing over with." Heuristics and poor group decision-making appear to have played a significant part in the choice to cross the Jago River immediately instead of waiting until morning. Edward and Dave drove this decision, and Jill and Greg "didn't object." If they had re-evaluated the situation, the group may have changed where, when, or how they crossed the river.

Use of the rope. The group did not have a plan for how the rope would be used in case of an accident. Roped river crossings are an advanced technique, with the potential to increase hazards if not executed skillfully. The taut rope, which angled upstream during the second half of the crossing, may have made it more difficult for Edward to make progress.

Failure to loosen the hip belt and sternum strap of the pack. The group had briefly discussed the merits and demerits of unbuckling their backpacks, but decided to leave them buckled for greater load stability. Experts generally recommend that hip belts and sternum straps be unbuckled during river crossings, so the pack can be jettisoned more easily in an emergency. (*Source: Compiled by Dick Dorworth, with input from the team members.*)

Editor's note: Links to educational resources on wilderness river crossings can be found in the online version of this report: publications.americanalpineclub.org.

CREVASSE FALL | Climbing Unroped
Hayes Range, Trident Glacier

Sarah Hart, 35, and I, 32, intended to climb the east ridge of 13,832-foot Mt. Hayes, the tallest peak in the eastern Alaska Range, from the Trident Glacier. The Trident was flat and windswept in April, and the snow surface was so hard that we didn't even leave footprints in the crust. We decided it would be fine to cross the glacier to the base of the ridge unroped.

I walked in front, wearing a harness, while Sarah walked behind me with the rope. It was Sarah's idea that whoever carried the rope should go second, in the unlikely event of a crevasse fall. I only made it a few hundred meters across the flat glacier from the tent before breaking through a hidden snow bridge and falling into a crevasse. I think I fell as much as 60 feet.

I was not wearing a helmet (as I was not expecting to fall in a crevasse) and I was knocked out in the fall. When I regained consciousness, Sarah was lowering me a rope. We were able to communicate, and she told me that she had a good anchor for me. Using a Petzl Tibloc and a prusik, I was able to climb out on my own.

We walked back to the tent and used a satellite phone to call our pilot for a pickup. We were safely back to the highway in few hours.

ANALYSIS

If you fall in a crevasse unroped, you messed up. There are a lot of dangers that are inherent to climbing, but this isn't one of them. My accident boiled down to complacency—I just thought that it would be fine. It wasn't, and my fall easily could have been fatal or resulted in a life-changing injury. I got lucky.

Though I could see evidence in the distance of crevasses running perpendicular to our path, I was certain they were either closed or well bridged along our path. There was no indication of the crevasse on the snow surface where I fell in. I believe that the high winds that blow through the dry, cold Hayes Range created an ideal environment for thin, weak bridges that sag very little. (Colin Haley had a similar accident in the St. Elias Range, and his report in Accidents 2014 has an excellent analysis and recommendations). In the future, particularly in dry climates, I will be far more careful.

Sarah Hart starting across the flat, windswept Trident Glacier. (The pair's base camp is visible to the right.) Her decision to carry the rope and trail behind her partner may have saved his life. However, roping up would have been a far safer practice. *Seth Adams*

In the fall, my shoulder popped out of its socket but immediately went back in (an old injury, but very painful when it happens), and attempting to climb out, without assistance, would have been an ordeal, at best. Sarah's decision to follow behind me with the rope—one good decision in a sea of bad ones—may have saved my life.

Sarah was able to assist me in passing the lip by lowering an end of the rope and hauling. She was very pleased with the Petzl Micro Traxion for use as an autoblocking pulley. Given that I found my prusik to be time-consuming and inconvenient for climbing out of the crevasse, I believe I will now carry a Tibloc and a Micro Traxion, or similar device, as my ascending and rescue kit, with the possibility of improvising a prusik as a backup.

A note on partner rescue: I weigh nearly 100 pounds more than Sarah does. Though we didn't do any hauling to test this, I believe there is no way she would have been able to haul me out on her own using a 3:1 mechanical advantage system. I believe the common practice of carrying two pulleys needs to be reassessed, since in many situations more mechanical advantage will be required.

Going forward, I will be far more cautious in my approach to glacier travel. When arriving at a new area, I'll spend more time probing to learn about the snowpack and the bridges. Though our decision to travel unroped on the glacier was contrary to well-accepted safe practices, I believe many people likely would have made the same decision—with the rationale that it would be "fine." I urge everyone not to be complacent with respect to such high-consequence decisions. (*Source: Seth Adams.*)

Editor's note: An interview with Seth Adams about this incident was featured in the debut episode of "The Sharp End" podcast, available at iTunes and Soundcloud.

HYPOTHERMIA AND EXPOSURE | Climbing Alone
Denali, West Buttress

On May 5, Javier Callupan, a 39-year-old male from Argentina, was observed moving from the 11,200-foot camp to the 14,200-foot camp on the West Buttress. On May 6 he moved from the 14,200-foot camp to high camp at 17,200 feet. All other parties attempting to move to high camp on this day turned around due to inclement weather.

On May 10, at 11:30 p.m., a call to the Talkeetna Ranger Station reported that members of a U.S. Coast Guard team had found a deceased individual next to the Park Service rescue cache at the 17,200-foot camp. This individual was later identified as Callupan. He was found lying on the surface of the snow with the fly of his tent partially draped around him.

The climber's body was recovered from 17,200 feet on May 29. The medical examiner's report indicated that Callupan died from hypothermia and exposure to the environment. [*Denali National Park Case Incident Record.*]

ANALYSIS
The climber moved up the mountain quicker than recommended—less than six days from base camp to high camp, including ascending from 11,200 feet to 17,200 feet in just two days. Moreover, the weather during this period was poor, with high winds, cold, and snow. It was likely a combination of exhaustion, altitude sickness, and difficult weather conditions that caused him to fail to set up his tent, leaving him susceptible to hypothermia. Early season attempts on the West Buttress Route require exceptional self-sufficiency, because few climbers will be on the route and ranger patrols generally do not reach the upper mountain until mid-May. (*Source: The Editors.*)

AVALANCHE | Stranded
Denali National Park, Ruth Gorge, Mt. Dickey, West Ridge

On May 11, at approximately 5:30 p.m., rangers received a call from K2 Aviation saying that one of their pilots had spotted an SOS stamped in the snow above 747 Pass (between Mt. Dickey and Mt. Bradley). Two climbers were present at the SOS and waving their arms for help. The pilot also reported ski tracks coming out of avalanche debris above them and a possible (unconfirmed) third climber in the debris.

A plan was made to send two rangers with a helicopter and a backup team in a fixed-wing aircraft. At 6:30 p.m., chopper 0AE launched from Talkeetna with rangers Tucker Chenoweth and Joseph McBrayer on board. The rangers were able to establish communication with the party via a radio that was delivered to the scene. It was reported back to the station that no one was missing and the two climbers had called for help because they were unable to descend safely from their location.

The helicopter went to a staging site to offload gear and make room for the climbers, who were picked up at 7:44 p.m. and flown to their campsite in the Ruth Gorge. (*Source: Denali National Park Case Incident Record and press release.*)

ANALYSIS

The two climbers, both in their 20s and from Idaho, triggered a large slab avalanche between 7,500 and 8,000 feet. The avalanche began in a shallow area of the slab but propagated widely, with an average crown depth of more than a meter. Neither climber was caught in the slide, which crossed hundreds of feet of their ascent track. The two searched for an escape route but were unable to find a way off the ridge without risking more avalanches. Their attempt on Dickey began soon af-

Climbers stranded by a large slab avalanche on the west ridge of Mt. Dickey. *NPS Photo | Tucker Chenoweth*

ter a large snowstorm (more than one meter of new snow at the 11,000-foot camp on Denali between May 8 and 10, with 15 inches reported at the 7,200-foot Kahiltna base). Waiting another day or two before climbing might have given the new snow time to stabilize. (*Source: The Editors and Denali Field Report blog.*)

FROSTBITE

Denali, West Buttress

On June 12, guide Michael Horst of Alpine Ascents International contacted rangers by radio to say he was attending to a patient with frostbite at 17,200 feet. The patient was stable and non-critical but had frostbitten all 10 fingers while setting up camp. Ranger Tucker Chenoweth, at 14,200 feet, consulted with Horst to facilitate basic care for frostbite. The following morning, Chenoweth and VIPs (Volunteers-in-Parks) Frank Prestion and Andrea Tupy climbed up to 16,200 feet. There they met the patient, who had descended with his own team from 17,200. Chenoweth lowered the patient down the fixed lines, while his team traveled down independently. At the bottom of the fixed lines, the patient, his team, and Chenoweth all roped together and descended to 14,200 feet and the NPS medical tent.

The patient's fingers were deemed to be unusable for his descent to base camp and a risk to himself and his team. The patient was flown from 14,200 camp by the NPS contract helicopter and released at base camp, and he flew out of the mountains via fixed-wing aircraft. (*Source: Denali National Park Case Incident Record.*)

ANALYSIS

Early recognition of the signs of frostbite is essential. Had the patient realized he was in danger and let his teammates finish the work of setting up camp, he might have minimized the damage. Practice essential climbing and camp skills while wearing gloves or mittens. Liner gloves can protect against contact with metal tent poles, fuel bottles, etc. (*Source: The Editors.*)

Editor's note: Another frostbite account from 2015 on Denali can be found at publications.americanalpineclub.org (search "Kodiak"). Here, you can also find "Essentials: Frostbite," by Denali ranger Dave Weber, first published in Accidents 2015.

HAPE, HACE
Denali, West Buttress

At approximately 11:30 a.m. on June 19, Ranger Joseph McBrayer's patrol at 17,200-foot camp was notified about a tent-bound climber presenting with a decreased level of responsiveness. Upon further investigation, it was discovered that the patient, a 26-year-old male of Japanese descent, had fallen ill approximately three days prior, upon arrival at high camp. According to his teammate, his condition had worsened throughout his stay at that elevation. Nevertheless, the day before the ranger patrol was contacted, the teammate had left the patient unattended in his tent while summiting Denali with another climbing party.

McBrayer and VIP Lance Taysom responded to the climber's tent and, following a complete patient assessment, determined he was likely suffering from high altitude pulmonary edema (HAPE). The patient met Denali National Park's emergency evacuation criteria, and a helicopter evacuation was requested.

The NPS contract helicopter, 0AE, was already en route to the Alaska Range for work projects, and this variable made for an efficient extrication of the critically ill patient. He was flown to base camp soon after 1 p.m. and transferred to a LifeMed helicopter at 1:35 p.m., then flown to Mat-Su Regional Medical Center in Palmer, where he was expected to spend two to three additional days in the ICU, recovering from a combination of HAPE and high altitude cerebral edema (HACE). (*Source: Denali National Park Case Incident Report.*])

ANALYSIS
For any severe high-altitude illness, descent is the definitive treatment. These climbers should have descended within a day or two after arriving at high camp, or as soon as the patient showed signs and symptoms of serious altitude sickness. Delay only decreases the chances of self-rescue and increases the chances of medical emergency. Leaving a stricken partner in such condition to make a summit bid transgresses the vary definition of partnership. (*Source: The Editors.*)

Editor's note: A report about another HAPE case on the West Buttress in 2015 can be found by searching "Polish MJ Expedition" at publications.americanalpineclub.org. In addition to the incidents described above, Denali rangers evacuated a climber with lower abdominal pain from 14,200 feet on the West Buttress, and a climber who tore his Achilles tendon was evacuated from the 11,200-foot camp. A team descending the Muldrow Glacier Route was evacuated after being unable to cross the McKinley River.

FALL ON SNOW | Climbing Unroped
Chugach State Park, Mt. Yukla

On January 18, 24-year-old Dasan Marshall fell to his death on the north face of 7,535-foot Mt. Yukla. He was attempting a variation of the route No Call No Show with 23-year-old Nikolai Windahl. (*Editor's note: No Call No Show is a serious,*

ESSENTIALS

HIGH ALTITUDE ILLNESS
PREVENTION, ASSESSMENT, & TREATMENT
By Dave Weber

High-altitude illness (HAI) occurs when climbers are exposed to the lower baro-metric pressure associated with elevation gain, resulting in insufficient oxygen available for absorption by the tissues of the body. When a climber is unable to effectively acclimate to a new altitude, signs and symptoms (S/S) of high-altitude illness can manifest. The effects can range from mild to life-threatening. Early recognition and treatment are essential to minimizing the severity of HAI. The following recommendations are based on the Wilderness Medical Society's Consensus Guidelines for the Prevention and Treatment of Acute Altitude Illness.

PREVENTION
In general, HAI initially affects climbers at elevations greater than 8,000 feet. When traveling to these altitudes, it is recommended that climbers increase their sleeping elevation by no more than 1,000 to 1,500 feet per day. If a route requires a larger elevation gain between camps, it is best to remain at one elevation for two or more days and travel to higher altitudes on day trips (hence the popular adage of "climb high and sleep low"). It is also best to incorporate a rest day, which includes light activity, following three to four consecutive days of increases in sleeping elevation.

Under physician direction, the medication acetazolamide (Diamox) can aid in acclimatization. Climbers at altitude should avoid any products that depress their innate respiratory drive, such as sedative medications and alcoholic beverages.

ASSESSMENT
HAI is typically delineated into three categories: acute mountain sickness (AMS), high altitude cerebral edema (HACE), and high altitude pulmonary edema (HAPE). AMS represents the mildest form of HAI, while HACE and HAPE are both severe presentations.

AMS occurs when non-acclimatized climbers ascend rapidly to altitude. HACE is severe AMC characterized by fluid accumulation (edema) within the brain, secondary to climbing at elevation. HAPE is also triggered by travel at high altitudes but is caused by excessive fluid within the lungs.

Acute Mountain Sickness
Headache accompanied by at least one of the following:
- Nausea (vomiting possible)
- Insomnia (difficulty sleeping)
- Fatigue
- Anorexia (loss of appetite)

High Altitude Cerebral Edema
- Ataxia (difficulties with gross motor movement, e.g. walking)

- Mental status changes (including disorientation, irritability, combativeness and/or unresponsiveness)
- Headache and other AMS S/S possible

High Altitude Pulmonary Edema
- Shortness of breath when resting
- Excessive fatigue
- Persistent cough (initially dry and becoming productive)

Note: Pulse oximetry (SpO2) monitors can be useful for monitoring an individual's oxygen saturation trend over time. However, no correlation has been found between SpO2 values and a climber's susceptibility to HAI.

FIELD TREATMENT

Acute Mountain Sickness

The most prudent treatment is to stop ascending, allowing the body to acclimatize, until signs and symptoms resolve. Rest days should be active, while maintaining appropriate nutrition and hydration. In addition:
- Consider acetazolamide (Diamox)*
- Treat symptoms (e.g. headache, nausea) with appropriate medication
- Supplemental oxygen can be administered if available
- Descend if patient is unable to acclimate or if S/S of HACE/HAPE present

High Altitude Cerebral Edema

The highest priority treatment is prompt descent until S/S resolve. In addition:
- Supplemental oxygen can be used if available
- Consider dexamethasone (Decadron)*
- Consider acetazolamide (Diamox)*
- Portable hyperbaric chamber can be used temporarily if descent isn't possible

High Altitude Pulmonary Edema

The highest priority treatment is prompt descent until S/S resolve. In addition:
- Supplemental oxygen should be used if available
- Consider inhaled albuterol (Ventolin)* and nifedipine (Procardia)*
- Portable hyperbaric chamber can be used temporarily if descent isn't possible

* Administration of any medications requires both wilderness medicine training and physician orders/protocols.

Note: HACE and HAPE can occur simultaneously and differential diagnosis can prove difficult. For this reason, some experts recommend initially treating severe HAI patients for both HACE and HAPE, until a diagnosis becomes clear.

HOSPITAL TREATMENT

Treatment of HAI in the clinical setting is similar to management in the field. Mountaineers suffering from the ill effects of altitude exposure often show improvement simply with transport to a lower elevation. Severe HAI patients should be assessed and monitored for any prolonged neurological and/or respiratory aftereffects associated with HACE/HAPE.

See the online version of this story (*publications.americanalpineclub.org*) for a list of resources and a link to the Wilderness Medical Society guidelines.

Dave Weber is a Denali mountaineering ranger and flight paramedic for Intermountain Life Flight.

20-pitch ice, snow, and mixed climb (5.6 WI5 M6), established in 2011.) The team had attempted another route on the face on January 17, but retreated due to spindrift coming down the route. They bivied that night at approximately 3,500 feet at the base of the valley. On the day of the accident, they began climbing at 6:30 a.m.

The team climbed unroped into a couloir, moving up moderate névé slopes (reaching 60°) and through a short overhanging section. After about three hours, they reached a 30-foot section of almost vertical snow and ice, which seemed to give way to more moderate terrain. Dasan was scouting a route through the steeper section, and he called down to Nikolai that it was difficult but doable. Immediately after this, at about 10 a.m., Dasan slipped and fell 1,000 feet down the face. Dasan died of a head injury caused by contact with rock while falling down the couloir. He was wearing a lightweight, foam mountaineering helmet.

Nikolai was forced to downclimb the route, as the party's rope was in Dasan's pack. While retreating, he had to improvise a rappel down a 20-foot overhanging section using a shovel blade as an anchor and 30 feet of 7mm cord. It took him about two hours to reach to Dasan. Nikolai assessed Dasan as deceased and attempted to call 911 with his cellular phone; poor cell reception caused his call to be dropped. Nikolai had to follow their tracks down the technical Icicle Creek drainage alone to find better cell reception. After descending for an hour, he was able to communicate the emergency to a friend in town via text message. He then continued his descent to the established trail and reached the trailhead at 4:30 p.m. A Para-

The north face of Mt. Yukla. The line attempted during the incident is near the center of the face. *Micah McGuire*

rescue team from the 212th Alaska Air National Guard, alerted by Nikolai's friend, recovered Dasan's body by helicopter around 4:30 the same afternoon.

ANALYSIS

Nikolai did not see the exact events leading to Dasan's slip, but it is reasonable to speculate that he lost his footing or ice tool placements in the snow and was unable to stop his fall. Nikolai was able to keep his focus and retreat from the climb, improvising with the minimal equipment he had. When a team decides to simul-solo in high-consequence terrain, splitting up the technical gear and ropes would give each climber more options for descending alone. Using half ropes instead of a single rope also gives better options for retreating.

Although it would not have changed the outcome of this accident, arranging for the use of a reliable satellite-based communication device would have allowed Nikolai to communicate his emergency earlier. (*Sources: Eeva Latosuo, Alaska Pacific University; Bill Billmeier, Alaska Mountaineering School; Nikolai Windahl.*)

ARIZONA

FALL ON ROCK | Lowering Error, Rope Too Short
The Pit, Son Tower

On a mid-September evening, Person 1, age 29, with many years of climbing experience, led the limestone sport climb Pleasant Dreams (5.9+) on Son Tower. When the leader reached the top of the climb, the belayer (Person 2, age 30, with six months of experience) began to lower him to the ground. At the second bolt from the bottom of the climb, Person 2 tried to stop the climber so he could clean a quickdraw. At that time, the belayer suddenly realized the rope was too short. The rope pulled through the belayer's device, and Person 1 fell approximately 20 feet to the ground, suffering abrasions and lacerations.

ANALYSIS
Person 1 had done the climb before and knew the 50-meter rope he was using was not long enough to lower a climber all the way to the bottom of the route. His plan was to stop on a ledge partway down and then scramble to the bottom of the climb. However, he forgot to stop on the ledge. Person 2 was focused on the climber and was not paying attention to how much rope remained.

Using a rope of appropriate length would have prevented this accident. In addition, closing the system by tying a knot at the end of the rope or tying the end to a rope bag to prevent it from feeding through the belay device could have provided an effective backup. (*Source: Aaron Dick, SAR Coordinator, Coconino County Sheriff's Office.*)

RAPPEL FAILURE | Inadequate Anchor
Tonto National Forest, Coon Bluff Recreation Area

In January, Arizona State University student Katelyn Conrad died after falling 125 to 150 feet to the ground while rappelling. Conrad, who had some climbing experience, and two other women were part of a group practicing rappelling techniques. The three women set up their rappel at the top of the cliff, and two of the women successfully completed single-strand rappels down the cliff face. When Conrad weighted the rope to begin her own rappel, the rope pulled free of the anchor and she fell to the ground, sustaining fatal injuries. (*Sources: News stories and online reports from eyewitnesses.*)

ANALYSIS
Based on eyewitness accounts, it is believed the accident was the result of a failed "biner block" rappel setup. The biner block is commonly used by canyoneers making long rappels, so they can use a single full-strength rope and then retrieve the rope by pulling on a much lighter cord. At the anchor, the rappel rope is tied to a carabiner that blocks the smaller rope from pulling through the anchor. (*See photo on next page.*)

When Conrad fell during her rappel, the full rope came down with her. The anchor (a sling around a large block with a "rapide," a.k.a. quick-link, rappel ring)

did not fail. A locked carabiner, used in the biner block setup, was found adjacent to the anchor.

In this instance, the climbers appear to have either (A) tied a clove hitch to the blocking carabiner that was poorly tied and/or poorly positioned such that it slipped and allowed the rope to pull through, or else (B, more likely) accidentally tied a Munter hitch instead of a clove hitch. The hitch held long enough for the first two women to rappel, and then shifted under Conrad's weight and released. There was no backup.

Although the biner block (and the related Reepschnur anchor setup) are useful techniques for certain situations, they should not be used in normal climbing or rappelling, where a standard double-rope rappel is preferred. Learning or practicing these specialty techniques should always be done under expert supervision. (*Source: The Editors, with information from eyewitness accounts.*)

A "biner brake" rappel anchor is most commonly used by canyoneers in order to rappel a single rope, which then can be retrieved by pulling a thin cord. The main rappel rope should be backed up to the anchor until the final person descends. Great care must be taken to tie the blocking knot correctly and ensure the carabiner cannot pull through the anchor.

FALL ON ROCK | Inadequate Protection
Mt. Lemmon, Windy Point

On May 25, a 32-year-old male climber leading Agatha Christie (5.8 trad) fell and pulled out one or more pieces of protection. He fell about 45 feet to the ground, sustaining broken bones and internal injuries. He was short-hauled from the scene and transferred to a Life Net air ambulance with non-life-threatening injuries.

ANALYSIS
This route is popular but is considered a sustained and somewhat tricky-to-protect lead. To ensure solid protection, trad leaders must become proficient with a variety of protection types (cams, nuts, micro-nuts, offsets). A great way to practice protection on tricky routes is to toprope the climb and mock-protect it with the safety of a toprope belay. (*Source: The Editors.*)

Editor's note: In addition to the Arizona incidents described above, accounts of a fall with injuries at the Overlook and a rockfall-caused rappelling accicent at Sycamore Falls (both near Flagstaff) can be found at publications.americanalpineclub.org.

CALIFORNIA

STRANDED | Darkness, Inexperience, Climbing Alone
Mt. Shasta, Avalanche Gulch–Casaval Ridge

On April 10 a male climber in his 20s attempted a solo ski ascent via Avalanche Gulch and Casaval Ridge. The weather was clear and the conditions ideal for such a trip. He started climbing at 4 a.m. and did not summit until 7 p.m. While descending, though it was still light out, he got disoriented. He had decided not to ski–he later said he couldn't get his skins off. He also mentioned that his GPS had stopped working. He decided to start glissading with his skis on his pack, but headed down the east side of the mountain. (Avalanche Gulch is on the south side.) While glissading, one of his skis fell off his pack. He was too tired to retrieve it and decided to leave his other ski too.

The climber ended up spending the night in an open bivy in the Mud Creek/Konwakiton Glacier area. He called 911 that night and also activated his SPOT device. Lead climbing ranger Nick Meyers, alerted to the situation at 2 a.m., tried numerous times to reach the climber without success. A plan was made to search for the climber the next morning. Early on April 11, Meyers reached the climber by phone, and through conversation and the SPOT device's signal, Meyers confirmed his location and talked him through walking over Sargents Ridge and down into the Old Ski Bowl. Meanwhile, Meyers asked for a California Highway Patrol (CHP) helicopter to fly over the area to confirm the climber's location and be available in case of injury. CHP spotted him on top of Sargents Ridge and picked him up from there. He suffered no injuries other than exhaustion and damaged pride–and the loss of a sweet pair of skis.

ANALYSIS
The climber was equipped with dual alpine ice axes with leashes, a harness, and various other top-notch gear. He was unfamiliar with the route and overburdened with his equipment. While it's great to be prepared, there is a line between having enough equipment and too much unnecessary gear. Better research and planning would have helped the climber pack the appropriate equipment for his adventure. Also, GPS units have limitations, including battery failure. One needs to have a map and compass, and the skills to use them, as backup. (*Source: Mt. Shasta Wilderness Climbing Ranger Report 2015.*)

Editor's note: Two other accounts of climbers losing their way on Shasta in 2015 can be found online. Search "Shastina saddle" and "nine lives" at publications.americanalpineclub.org.

FALL ON SNOW | Failure to Self-Arrest
Mt. Shasta, Avalanche Gulch

Michael Murphy, in his mid-50s, was climbing the Avalanche Gulch Route with partners early the morning of June 11. They reached the Red Banks and decided to turn around. They had begun descending when, at about 12,400 feet, Murphy caught his crampons on the cuff of his pants, tripped, and slid 2,000 feet down the route. The snow at the time was very smooth and firm.

A guided Sierra Wilderness Seminars team was on the route and witnessed the fall. They quickly descended to where Murphy came to rest. Two of the clients on the trip were ER doctors from San Francisco. Impressively, they were able to perform a tracheotomy using a CamelBak hose and bladder, and though the patient was unconscious, the off-duty doctors were able to establish an airway. When a helicopter arrived and hoisted him into the ship, the patient reportedly was breathing, but the rescuers were not able to sustain life. This was the first fatality on the mountain since 2011.

ANALYSIS

Descending on firm snow can be tedious and potentially dangerous on steep slopes, and it's possible for any climber to trip on the cuff of one's pants. (Slim-fitting pants and/or gaiters help minimize this risk.) The climber tripped and likely fell headfirst and rapidly gained speed—a difficult position in which to initiate self-arrest. Reports said he was knocked unconscious during his fall, which may have contributed to his lack of self-arrest. He was wearing a helmet, but it's not known if it was secured properly. He also was reported to have a pacemaker, though this is not suspected as a direct contributing factor to the accident. (*Source: Mt. Shasta Wilderness Climbing Ranger Report 2015.*)

AVALANCHE | Poor Position

Mt. Shasta, Hotlum-Wintun Route

On June 13, near the Hotlum-Wintun Route on the east side of Shasta, a male climber triggered a loose-wet avalanche at about 13,000 feet while glissading. The climber involved had separated from his group at around 3 p.m. and met a group of skiers who were descending from the summit. The skiers recom-

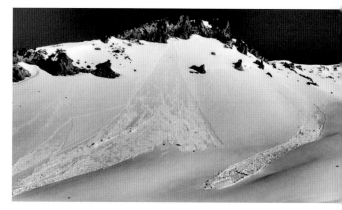

Point-release avalanches can be triggered by falling rock or ice, snow "rollers," climbers, or skiers. They typically fan out and entrain more snow as they slide. *Bob Hutcheson*

mended the climber turn around due to the late hour. The climber agreed and quickly prepared to glissade. The slope the individual intended to glissade was a bit steeper than the route of ascent, and the snow was quite soft due to the hour of the day and warm, summer-like temperatures.

Shortly after the climber started his glissade, a point-release, loose-wet avalanche was triggered. It gained speed and entrained a considerable amount of snow and the climber. The avalanche grew to an estimated 150–200 feet wide and traveled close to 1,200 feet. The climber tried to use his axe to self-arrest, but was unable to stop. When the avalanche came to a rest, the climber managed to stay on top of the debris, but he had been battered by debris within the slide and sustained what—at the time—were considered minor injuries. He was able to self-rescue by gingerly hiking 4,000 feet down and three miles to the Brewer Creek trailhead. A visit to the hospital revealed two hairline femur fractures and a large contusion.

ANALYSIS

Spring and early summer conditions on Mt. Shasta, while seemingly benign, can present several dangerous factors. Cold nights create firm snow in the morning, which can lead to long falls should one slip and fail to self-arrest. On the other hand, warm nights and hot days can exacerbate rockfall and make for very soft snow surfaces, resulting in loose-wet, point-release avalanches. Midafternoon sun on warm easterly and southerly aspects presents the most favorable conditions for loose-wet snow instability. These slides start small but can quickly grow as they move downhill. A skier, glissading climber, or rockfall can easily start a loose-wet slide and sweep a person into rocks, over a cliff, or into a crevasse.

This climber should be commended for his self-rescue. Mt. Shasta is in close proximity to urban areas, but climbers need to remember that timely rescue is not always an option. Climbers should carry the proper equipment and have the appropriate skills to handle an emergency situation on their own. (*Source: Mt. Shasta Wilderness Climbing Ranger Report 2015.*)

FALL ON SNOW | Glissading With Crampons
Mt. Shasta, Avalanche Gulch

On June 16 a female climber was descending the Avalanche Gulch Route with crampons on her boots. While glissading just below the Red Banks, at about 12,000 feet, both of her crampons caught in the snow, breaking her ankles and taking her for a good tumble. Other climbers splinted her ankles with ski poles, and a team of six helped her down the mountain. She was approximately 600 vertical feet above the Lake Helen ranger base camp when climbing ranger Matt Dooley arrived on scene.

The climber was in stable condition, with strong vital signs, but had sore ribs and could not bear weight on her feet. It was decided that a helicopter should be ordered due to the likelihood of two broken ankles. Dooley placed the climber on a short rope and assisted the team in getting her to Lake Helen base camp. A California Highway Patrol helicopter arrived at about 4 p.m. and flew her off the mountain.

ANALYSIS

The Mt. Shasta rangers constantly stress that climbers never should glissade while wearing crampons. Regardless, a few slip through the cracks. Double broken ankles should teach a powerful lesson. (*Source: Mt. Shasta Wilderness Climbing Ranger Report 2015.*)

Editor's note: In May, a climber called for a helicopter evacuation after falling at around 9,400 feet while descending Avalanche Gulch. After confirming his injury was not life-threatening and that he had both the equipment and climbing partners for a safe night out, rangers denied the helicopter request and advised the party that rescue personnel would respond in the morning. A Siskiyou County SAR team assisted the climber, who had a mildly twisted knee, to walk off the mountain under his own power the next day.

FALL ON SNOW OR ICE
Mt. Shasta, Hotlum-Bolam Route

At approximately 10 a.m. on October 10, rangers Forrest Coots and Matt Dooley received a radio transmission reporting a climber (male, mid-20s) with a broken ankle on the Hotlum-Bolam Route. The climber reportedly fell above 12,000 feet on an ice sheet and tumbled some distance; his crampon eventually snagged and broke his ankle. His climbing partners retrieved a tent and sleeping bag from their campsite at 10,500 feet and sheltered the injured climber until help could arrive.

A California Highway Patrol helicopter was requested and available; however, gusty 50–60 mph winds prevented the helicopter from picking up the injured person. Coots and Dooley coordinated with Siskiyou County SAR, and at 1:45 p.m. they tied in with three members of the SAR team and started climbing toward the injured party. At

Rescuers carry an injured climber with a broken ankle down from 12,000 feet on Mt. Shasta. They reached the road at 4:30 a.m. *Matt Dooley*

5:30 p.m., after three miles of steep climbing, the rescue team arrived on scene at 12,000 feet, higher than originally reported. Their location was on a scree ridge in the Bolam Glacier area. Coots assessed the climber and confirmed a broken ankle, then splinted and stabilized the injury. The team decided to get the injured climber down to the 10,000-foot base camp and reassess.

At 6 p.m. the team began their descent with the injured climber in a soft litter. The terrain was very rough and high winds made travel very slow. At 10 p.m. the team reached base camp, and Coots and Dooley decided to keep descending with the climber, with the help of the SAR team. An hour later, at 9,500 feet, the team was able to transfer the climber into a hard litter brought up by another SAR team and continue the descent. At 1:30 a.m. the rescue team reached a wheeled litter and continued toward the Northgate parking lot, which they reached at 4:30 a.m. The climber was transferred to the hospital by ambulance.

ANALYSIS
The injured climber was fortunate to have strong, able partners who could call for a rescue and care for the climber until help arrived. The rescuers made a good decision to continue the arduous descent throughout the night, getting the injured climber to the hospital as soon as possible. The doctors said if he had been out

much longer, they might have had to amputate the foot due to vascular complications. (*Sources: Mt. Shasta Wilderness Climbing Ranger Report 2015 and Siskiyou County SAR.*)

Editor's note: 5,679 summit passes were sold for Mt. Shasta in 2015, an 18 percent increase over the previous year. Climbing rangers performed six rescues, three searches, and two assists with minor injuries or self-rescue. All but one of the incidents occurred during the descent, and more than half involved climbers with little or no mountaineering experience.

FALL ON ROCK AND SNOW | Inexperience, Off Route
Sawtooth Range, Cleaver Peak

On March 21 the Mineral County Sheriff (Nevada) received a 911 call from Brandon Reiff (33) of Reno, who reported that he had broken his leg in a fall near Matterhorn Peak (12,280 feet). His 911 call was transferred to the Mono County Sheriff, but the call was dropped due to poor reception. Attempts to re-establish contact were unsuccessful, so his exact whereabouts were unknown.

Mono County SAR responded, along with a helicopter from the California Highway Patrol. Due to high winds, the helicopter had limited capability for searching near the 12,000-foot peak, so a larger helicopter was requested. Just prior to dark, the subject was spotted at approximately 10,000 feet on a steep slope below the crest of ridgeline forming Cleaver Peak (11,760'), two miles north of Matterhorn Peak. The helicopter tried numerous times to lower a medic but was unsuccessful due to high winds, the steep slope, and darkness.

That evening Mono County SAR personnel began hiking to the subject's location. A larger helicopter and assistance from the Inyo County SAR team were requested for the morning of March 22. While SAR personnel climbed to the victim's location, a Chinook helicopter was able to lower a crewman. The climber was hoisted up to the helicopter, then flown to Bryant Field in Bridgeport. (*Source: Mono County SAR.*)

ANALYSIS

In late winter or early spring, any route on Matterhorn Peak or Cleaver Peak is a mountaineering objective, involving a considerable amount of steep snow climbing and exposed, steep, and possibly snow-covered rock. Although this climber's equipment included mountaineering boots, crampons, a climbing helmet, and an appropriate clothing system for winter mountaineering—but no ice axe—he did not have technical mountaineering skills or experience.

According to the climber, he made the decision to attempt Matterhorn Peak late the night before and did not leave the trailhead until after 8:30 a.m. He was unable to locate the trail toward the peak; instead, he chose to scramble and bushwhack up a streambed toward the mountain. After realizing he had underestimated the approach to Matterhorn Peak, he decided to attempt Cleaver Peak instead, without foreknowledge of any route. He climbed the snow slope up to the ridgeline forming Cleaver Peak with crampons. Once reaching the steep rock walls on Cleaver's northeast side, he continued upward but soon realized the terrain necessitated rock climbing equipment, and so he began downclimbing.

A climber on Pine Line at the foot of the Nose. The Pine Line belay is on the tree ledge above the climber. The normal belay for the first pitch of the Nose is higher and around the corner to the right. *Ben Lyon*

While negotiating a steep section, the climber decided to let go and drop a short distance to a ledge below. Upon impact with the ledge, the climber broke his leg and went into a free fall down rock cliffs and snow slopes, eventually coming to a stop on a snowbank. He placed a call to 911 and attempted to splint his leg. The climber noted he'd also dislocated his left shoulder and broken multiple ribs; he also had pain and swelling on the back of his head and neck. Due to his injuries and the difficulty of rescue, the climber spent a full night out in single-digit temperatures and was lucky to survive without additional cold injuries.

What can novice mountaineers take away from this?

Plan ahead. Knowledge of the route and general area is important to success and survival.

Leave early. Most individuals attempting high peaks in winter, or under winter conditions, depart in the predawn hours.

Have the right equipment. In this terrain the climber should have been using an ice axe in conjunction with his crampons. With a rope and rock climbing protection—and the knowledge to use it—the climber could have built anchors and facilitated a safer descent. (*Source: The Editors, with information from a blog post by the climber.*)

FALL ON ROCK | Inadequate Protection
Yosemite Valley, El Capitan, The Nose

On May 9, at approximately 9:30 a.m., YOSAR dispatch received a call about an injured climber who had taken a 20-foot leader fall on the first pitch of the Nose. As YOSAR mobilized to El Cap Meadow, a ranger at the base of Pine Line (a 5.7 crack just below the start of the Nose) indicated that the injured climber's partners were belaying around the corner from the victim, anchored to the pine tree at the top of Pine Line. The ranger also said that another team, which had been waiting to start the Nose, was assisting the climbers and had fixed a line from the top of Pine Line to the ground.

One member of the assisting team was able to clip the injured climber into their system and rappel with the injured climber, who was ambulatory, down to the base. Shortly after the injured climber had reached the ground, YOSAR arrived on scene with a litter team. They loaded the injured climber into the litter and wheeled him out to El Cap Meadow, where the climber was transferred to a medical helicopter.

There were a couple of contributing factors in this incident. First, after completing Pine Line, most parties will move the belay around a corner to the ledge beneath the first pitch of the Nose before starting that route. This decreases the potential for rope drag on the leader, and better communication can be maintained between belayer and leader. The leader was leapfrogging two cams on the first pitch of the Nose (5.10d or C1) when both pieces, for whatever reason, came out of the crack; no other gear was in position to protect the climber, and he fell to the ledge at the start of the pitch. In this case, additional protection may not have prevented the ledge fall, due to rope stretch. However, if you're going to leapfrog gear, it's a good idea to leave sufficient protection in place to prevent a dangerous fall. (*Source: NPS ranger Brandon Latham.*)

FALL ON ROCK | Off-Route
Yosemite Valley, Manure Pile Buttress

On May 16, after several days of rain in Yosemite Valley, the cliffs were busy and all the routes at Manure Pile were occupied except for an obscure moderate climb. We decided to be adventurous and climb it anyway, as its grade was well below our ability level. On the second pitch I got slightly off-route, committed to a difficult move well above the last available gear, and then a handhold broke. My final piece of protection was good, but I was just too far above it. The protection may have helped absorb my fall, but I still hit a ledge below, hard. The fall was roughly 25 feet in all.

The front and back of my helmet took a serious impact in the fall; it definitely saved my head. Initially I felt dizzy and believed I had broken a rib and possibly my tailbone. My partner and I discussed calling for a rescue, but I felt I could get off the climb under my own power and we self-rescued, with my partner controlling my rappel. He helped me to the car and drove me to the hospital, where CT and MRI scans confirmed a minor concussion, three fractured vertebrae, and other spinal injuries.

ANALYSIS
We were too eager to climb. Rather than waiting for a higher quality route to open up or going to a different area, we climbed a route that wasn't well-traveled or as safe. I'm thankful that my helmet protected me adequately. (*Source: Anonymous 28-year-old male.*)

RAPPEL ERROR
Yosemite, El Capitan, The Nose

On May 27, five climbers had gathered near Camp VI on the Nose—a team of two and a team of three had been climbing alongside each other over the previous days. A member of the team of three was leading midway up the Changing Corners pitch, above Camp VI, when a piece of gear dropped and landed on a small ledge, roughly 25 feet below Camp VI. In a quick conversation, Tyler Gordon, a member of the team of three, decided to rappel to the gear and retrieve it. The team witnessed Gordon lean back and then fall from the Camp VI ledge. He fell to the end of the rope, landing at Camp V.

The leader immediately lowered to Camp VI and then continued to Camp V. It was obvious to him that Gordon had died from injuries sustained in the fall, and the leader called YOSAR to initiate assistance with the recovery. A team of rescuers was flown to the top of El Cap, along with 2,400 feet of rope and equipment to rig two lines for accessing Camp V, which is roughly 1,000 feet below the rim. Two lower and raise operations were completed just before darkness to get the team off the wall.

ANALYSIS

In an accident like this, it can be hard to determine exactly what happened. To the best of the team's knowledge, Gordon unclipped from his tie-in point at the anchor before falling from the Camp VI ledge. His belay device, a Grigri, was seen clipped to his harness and closed shut, so he either fell before attaching the device to the rope or assumed the device was rigged properly when it was not.

As climbers we often change our personal anchor or tie-in when switching locations at ledges, rigging rappels, changing over from jugging to belaying, or trying to clean up clusters at belays. On big walls, after days of hanging in a harness, ledges become places to relax—and thus may lead to moments of inattention. Whenever you switch from one point of attachment to another (for example, from the anchor to a rappel device), make sure that you are secure on your next attachment before unclipping. It is good practice to check untested systems with a backup before committing to them. Look out for your partners too. (*Source: NPS ranger Brandon Latham.*)

RAPPEL ERROR | Darkness
Yosemite Valley, Washington Column

On October 30, at approximately 8:45 p.m., Yosemite Dispatch received a report that a climber, Ethan Gillett, had fallen 100 to 200 feet from the South Face Route (V 5.8 C1) on Washington Column and landed on Dinner Ledge. Another climber, a Wilderness First Responder, confirmed that Gillett was unresponsive, not breathing, and pulseless and had sustained injuries not compatible with life. Based on this report, park medical control concurred that Gillett was deceased and a recovery operation was delayed until the next morning. The other climbers at Dinner Ledge—seven in all, including Gillett's partner, Joshua Schultz—decided to rappel off that night, leaving behind fixed lines to Dinner Ledge. A small team of rescuers hiked to the base of the route to help them down to the valley floor.

The next morning the recovery team climbed to Dinner Ledge. Gillett lay about 20 feet up and left of the main part of the ledge, in a group of large boulders near the start of the route Southern Man. He was wearing a helmet and a rappel glove on his right hand. A Grigri was attached to the belay loop of his harness via a locked auto-locking carabiner. There was no indication of incorrect rigging.

The previous day Schultz and Gillett had climbed the first three pitches of the South Face to Dinner Ledge. They bivouacked there and, according to Schultz, began climbing the remaining eight pitches to the summit the morning of the incident, leaving their bivy gear at Dinner Ledge. After topping out near sunset, they began rappelling the route, intending to retrieve their gear and continue to the base in the dark. This is a common strategy for parties not wanting to haul gear up the route; it also avoids the slippery scramble with large packs down North Dome Gully, the alternate descent from the summit.

Schultz was having problems with his headlamp so Gillett went first in order to find the rappel stations using his functioning headlamp. When they reached the anchor for pitch six they found fixed lines belonging to a party that was now bivouacked on Dinner Ledge, two rappels below. Gillett yelled down to the climbers, asking for permission to use their fixed lines, and the climbers agreed. Gillett and Schultz coiled their ropes and began rappelling a fixed blue rope. Gillett went first to the pitch five anchor, followed by Schultz.

As Schultz arrived at the pitch five anchor, Gillett stated, "Alright, I am going to rap," and he began rappelling another fixed blue rope. Shortly thereafter, Schultz heard him yell briefly, followed by a loud crash a couple of seconds later. Schultz called to Gillett. There was no response, but a voice on Dinner Ledge said, "CPR." He pulled up the blue line Gillett had rappelled and discovered that it was only a 40-foot, unknotted tail strand of the same blue rope they had just used to rappel pitch six; this rope had been tied off at the pitch five anchor, leaving the strand hanging below.

Schultz realized Gillett must have rappelled off the end of the rope. He found another rope fixed at the same anchor, white in color, and asked the climbers on Dinner Ledge if it reached them. They responded affirmatively, so he rappelled this line to the ledge.

ANALYSIS

Fixed lines are common on popular wall routes in Yosemite. They can make your descent faster, easier, and even comforting, giving you a sense of being home before you get there. But those factors also breed complacency, leading to shortcuts in procedure and loss of discipline. We don't know what went through Gillett's mind as he started his final rappel, but it's clear that he missed some steps—steps that were especially important in the dark. Had he noticed that the rope below him was unusually lightweight, or asked the climbers on Dinner Ledge to confirm the rope reached them, or paused to check the rope below him as he rappelled, this accident might have been prevented. (*Sources: NPS rangers Brandon Latham and John Dill.*)

STRANDED | Climbing Alone
Yosemite Valley, El Capitan, Tangerine Trip

On June 17, Yosemite Search and Rescue responded to a 6 a.m. request for help from a solo climber on pitch 15 of Tangerine Trip (VI 5.7 A3/C3). He reported that he had lost partial use of both hands and that completing the climb was no longer viable. The climber had previously taken a full rest day, hoping this would resolve the problem, but the issue persisted and he made the decision that assistance was needed. Up to this point, he had been on the wall for seven days.

YOSAR mobilized at 7 a.m. Once in position at the top of the Trip, a spotter in El Cap Meadow assisted the team in establishing a line down to the climber's position. A rescuer was lowered to the climber to help him secure his equipment in a haul bag and break down his portaledge. After the climber's injuries were assessed

YOSAR team works on top of El Capitan to raise a climber stranded on Tangerine Trip. *Drew Smith*

and equipment secured, the climber and rescuer were raised to the top of El Cap.

Rescuers descended with the climber, walking down to the top of the East Ledges. Due to the nature of the climber's injuries, he was lowered down a couple of steep sections of the descent, and a series of assisted lowers was conducted down the standard East Ledges rappels.

ANALYSIS

Climbing El Cap solo is obviously far more difficult than climbing in a team. Running into issues alone can immediately halt your progress and leave you stranded. In this case, the injuries to the climber's hands could have led to more serious injuries while trying to climb out or descending on his own. Careful consideration of contingency plans while solo climbing is always prudent, including carrying extra food and water for unplanned situations. (*Source: NPS ranger Brandon Latham.*)

FALL ON ROCK | Inadequate Protection
Yosemite Valley, El Capitan, Lurking Fear

On September 19, at approximately 5:30 p.m., YOSAR was notified about a climber who had taken a 15-meter fall on Lurking Fear. The climber suffered serious injuries, including possible head trauma. The reporting party was another climbing team on Lurking Fear.

With the use of a spotting scope, members of YOSAR were able to locate the injured party around pitch 14. Using a megaphone and hand signals, contact was made with the partner of the injured climber. The partner confirmed the injured climber potentially had a broken clavicle and had not lost consciousness. Given the late hour and the perception that the injured climber had not lost consciousness, it was decided that rescue operations would be postponed until the following morning.

At 7 a.m. the following day, the park's helicopter was brought in for a recon flight. (It's hard to assess Lurking Fear from the ground.) It was determined that a top-down rescue would be very difficult and potentially more hazardous for rescue personnel than a short-haul mission using the helicopter.

The helicopter took off with a rescuer hanging underneath and inserted him at the location of the injured climber. A second rescuer was then inserted with a litter, and the two rescuers packaged the patient for a pick-off. The helicopter circled back and retrieved the patient, two rescuers, and a substantial amount of the climbers' gear. From El Cap Meadow, the injured climber was transferred to an ambulance. The partner of the injured climber joined another climbing team and continued to the top.

ANALYSIS

After speaking with the injured climber, it was determined that direct aid was being used at the time of the fall. The last thing the leader remembers is placing a micro-cam and stepping into an aider to weight it. Speaking with other climbers at the scene, it appears this top piece blew and the climber proceeded to pull at least two more pieces of protection before being caught by a number four Camalot. After the fall, the belayer was able to lower the climber to a ledge and then descend to the injured leader to assist.

The placement of multiple questionable pieces of protection in a row was perhaps the main contributing factor to this accident. While we don't know for sure if the climber had been back-cleaning protection, it's a good idea to leave solid pro at regular intervals, especially on harder terrain or above ledges. In this accident, the leader was starting off a large, tiered ledge system that he may have impacted during the fall.

Whereas megaphone communications had led YOSAR to believe the climber had not lost consciousness, adjacent climbers said in follow-up interviews that the injured climber was going in and out of consciousness, and that the climber's helmet was severely deformed. (See "Essentials: Head Injuries" in Accidents 2015 or at publications.americanalpineclub.org for important information about identifying, assessing, and treating head injuries.) We are reminded of how helpful helmets can be in preventing serious head trauma: According to medical personnel on the scene, it is very likely the patient's head injuries would have been much more substantial had he not been wearing one. (Source: Yosemite ranger Eric Bissell.)

FALL ON ROCK | Inadequate Protection, Inexperience
Yosemite Valley, Leaning Tower, West Face

On September 27 at 8:25 a.m., 911 received a call from a climber on the west face of Leaning Tower, reporting another climber's fall. At the time, the injured lead climber was hanging unconscious 10 feet below Guano Ledge, after taking a lead fall of approximately 20 feet near the start of the fourth pitch.

YOSAR mobilized two teams: a climbing team to start ascending the route to Guano Ledge, and a top-down team prepared for a 1,200-foot lower with litter to package the climber and continue to the ground. A group of six was inserted just below the summit of the west face at Dano Ledge (pitch eight); without a landing zone atop Leaning Tower, it was necessary to insert the team using short-haul shuttles. From there, a park ranger and litter were lowered to within 40 feet of the climbers. The ranger tossed a beanbag-weighted pull cord to the climbers in order to be hauled into their position on this very overhanging wall.

The injured climber was packaged into the litter at 12:20 p.m., lowered to the ground, and flown from the base of Leaning Tower to El Cap Meadow. The partner of the injured climber rappelled to the ground with the YOSAR climbing team, and the YOSAR members still at the summit descended via the Leaning Tower Chimney. A visit to the hospital revealed no major injuries. The climber was released the same day.

A YOSAR team arrives just below the top of Leaning Tower to begin setting up 1,200-foot lowering systems. *Cheyne Lempe*

ANALYSIS

A follow-up interview was conducted with the partner of the injured climber. The two climbers were on their first climbing trip in the Valley. Both had five years of climbing experience, including three years of trad experience, and had climbed together before. Leaning Tower was their first attempt at a big wall and first aid climb. They said it seemed like a good introductory wall because the route looks like it was "mostly bolt ladders" on the topo.

The accident occurred on the team's second day of climbing, after sleeping on the popular Ahwahnee Ledge, left of Guano Ledge. The climbers had spent the night alongside a soloist and also noticed a second soloist coming up the pitch below Guano Ledge as they began climbing the second morning. From Guano Ledge, the leader clipped a bolt as the first piece of protection before making a pendulum to the right, around a right-facing corner, to access a thin crack. The leader proceeded to aid up the crack without leaving any gear for protection, as the climbers were concerned about rope drag after the pendulum. As the leader stood in his aiders on a micro-cam, the belayer remembers hearing a "pop" and seeing the climber swing sideways, back around the corner, and fall below Guano Ledge.

Although it's counterintuitive, a swinging pendulum fall is often more dangerous than a vertically oriented leader fall, due to fall force and terrain to smash into. When the micro-cam the leader was standing on pulled out, he was pulled off balance as he swung back left. A few right-facing corners created features to impact during the swing, and he appeared to hit the back of his head during the fall, beneath the rim of his helmet.

The belayer noted that the climbers had been anxious to move quickly that morning because of the other parties on the wall, and that the leader was potentially moving faster than he would have otherwise. On popular walls like the west face of Leaning Tower, the Nose of El Cap, and the south face of Washington Column, you will often see multiple parties of different experience levels sharing bivies and belays. Sometimes it is important to move quickly past bottlenecks of climbing parties, but other times it is better to slow down and let other teams to pass. Conversely, if it looks like your team's progress is contributing to stress for another climbing team, communicate with that team to make sure everyone can proceed safely.

The leader avoided clipping protection after the pendulum in order to avoid rope drag on the pitch. There are many locations where it may seem better to "walk" cams after a pendulum in order to avoid creating a "Z" in the rope. Using long runners can be effective in reducing rope drag in these situations. If there is no way to extend your placements for reduced drag, one could climb up, clipping gear along the way, then lower off solid protection to back-clean the problematic placement(s).

The belayer also commented that the climbers may not have been bounce-testing their placements regularly. While free climbing it is rare to test placements beyond a quick tug; however, when aid climbing it's a good idea to test most placements. Had this climber bounce-tested the micro-cam from below while still weighting his lower piece, he may have discovered the cam placement was not adequate before trusting it as his sole protection. (Source: Yosemite ranger Eric Bissell. The online version of this report includes a more comprehensive account of the events and analysis of the accident.)

FALL ON ROCK | Inadequate Anchor Tether, Inexperience
Yosemite Valley, Half Dome

Around sunset on November 7, Angela Uys (26) was at an anchor on Snake Dike (III 5.7), preparing to rappel. Her tether system was not effectively clipped to the anchor, and when she weighted the system it failed. She fell approximately 500 feet to her death.

At 9 that morning, Angela, Mason Kropp, and Samantha (Sam) Perry started up the Mist Trail toward Snake Dike. They were behind schedule because Angela had not arrived at their campsite in Yosemite Valley until 3 a.m., due to commitments in San Francisco. When they reached the base of the route, around 11:30 a.m., another party of three was climbing the first pitch.

At 1 p.m., after waiting 1.5 hours for the other party to clear, Mason began to lead the first pitch. Sam led the second, and Mason led the third. They were climbing with a single 70m rope, with Mason and Sam on opposite ends. Angela was attached to the middle of the rope with a figure 8 on a bight, clipped to a locking carabiner on her harness' belay loop.

For her anchoring system, Angela had girth-hitched a Metolius Personal Anchor System (PAS) to her belay loop. She had extended the free end of the PAS by girth-hitching to it one end of a 44-inch Metolius Rabbit Runner (a runner with a sewn loop on each end). She clipped the free end of the runner to the anchors with a locking carabiner and clipped the rope to the anchor as her backup. She reasoned that this extended configuration would allow her to stay well below the anchor, thus providing more space for the leader and belayer.

The sun was setting behind Glacier Point as Mason finished leading the third pitch. At that point they decided to rappel, given the late hour, the slow party ahead of them, and the possibility of a difficult, icy descent. None of them had climbed Snake Dike or descended Half Dome before.

After reaching the third-pitch anchors, Mason decided they should rappel from an alternate anchor 20 feet below and to climber's right of his location. The alternate anchor had rappel rings and was closer to the next anchor they would use on their retreat. Mason asked Angela to climb to the alternate anchor, clip in, and then unclip from the rope so that he could belay Sam up to join her.

Mason remembers looking down and seeing that Angela had not clipped a loop of the PAS into the anchor using a locking carabiner, as he had expected. As he recalls, she placed a locker on the anchor, but from his position it appeared she had threaded the end of the sling/PAS through the locker and closed the loop by clipping it back to her harness. It did not look like she had captured one of the sewn loops of the PAS on the anchor locker. As Sam climbed toward Angela's position, they heard her scream and watched as she tumbled down the rock face. They yelled for the party just above them to call 911.

Half Dome from the southwest. Snake Dike climbs the lower-angle face above the forested shoulder in the foreground. *David Iliff, License: CC-BY-SA 3.0*

Mason and Sam rappelled as fast as they could. On the way down they saw that a locker was still attached to one bolt of the anchor Angela was using. There was nothing else left at the anchor. In his haste to get to the ground, Mason rappelled off the end of the rope on his last rappel. He fell about 10 feet and twisted his ankle. He found Angela below and climber's right of the base of the climb. He checked for a pulse, but she was clearly dead.

ANALYSIS

Mason and Sam each had five to seven years of trad-climbing experience, but Angela had limited outdoor experience, with only a few trad leads, and she was still learning the techniques involved.

After her fall Angela's PAS/runner system was still girth-hitched to her harness. The free end of the runner was loose with no carabiner clipped to it. Two locking carabiners were clipped to her belay loop. One, unlocked, had probably been used to clip into the midpoint of the lead rope. The other was clipped through the two loops of her PAS closest to her harness. The gate was open and the locking sleeve was screwed into the locked position, which prevented the gate from closing.

Broken 5/16-inch bolt from the Owens River Gorge and remains of the placement. *Kevin Calder (top); Dan McDevitt (bottom)*

At the anchor from which she fell, Angela attempted to clip into only one bolt with a single anchoring system before detaching herself from the rope. A fundamental principle of anchoring is redundancy. In this instance, having a separate sling independently clipped between her harness and a bolt would likely have prevented her death. Angela had clipped in to the second- and third-pitch anchor with her rope and the PAS/sling combo, providing redundancy. Perhaps because of haste, fatigue, or lack of training, she did not choose to create a backup at this anchor. Angela was new to multi-pitch climbing, and the team's plan left her alone for the transition from being clipped to the rope to being attached to the anchor. Her faulty anchoring system may have been caught if one of the other climbers had been at the same anchor.

Other factors may have contributed to the accident, including lack of sleep and distraction. Mason and Sam said Angela had taken many photos with her iPhone during the climb. She had the phone in her hand, presumably to take a photo, at the time she fell.

With the available evidence, we can only speculate about the exact mechanism for Angela's anchoring system failure. But the factors above increased the possibility of a critical incident. During the first week of climbing we learn about redundant anchor systems, and we must continue to use them. Regardless of experience level, watch what your partner is doing. If you see something that doesn't look right, speak up! (*Source: Ranger Jesse McGahey.*)

FALL ON ROCK, BOLT FAILURE | Climbing Alone
Owens River Gorge, Silent Pillar Wall

Scott Sederstrom (44) fell to his death on March 13 when a bolt failed on Life in Electric Larvae Land (5.10b) at Silent Pillar Wall in the Owens River Gorge. When Sederstrom did not return from climbing that evening, his fiancée drove to the Lower Gorge parking lot, where she found his van and dog. Inyo Country Search and Rescue began an organized search in the morning. About an hour into the search, a family friend of Sederstrom's found his body at the base of the climb. Sederstrom was on the ground, with a stick clip attached to his harness and an eight-foot loop of slack between the tie-in point on his harness and the Grigri attached to his belay loop. A quickdraw was on the rope within the loop, with a bolt hanger (missing its bolt) clipped to the other end of the quickdraw. The evidence suggests that Sederstrom was using the stick clip to go bolt to bolt—unclipping the bolt below as he went and using the Grigri to ascend the short loop of rope to the bolt above him—when the third bolt on the climb failed. A Mini Traxion device was found in his pack, suggesting he was planning to set up a fixed line for top-rope soloing. Sederstrom fell 25 to 30 feet to the ground, suffering trauma to his head. He was not wearing a helmet. (*Sources: Rock and Ice, Dan McDevitt, Marty Lewis, and Greg Barnes.*)

ANALYSIS

The bolt in question was a 5/16-inch buttonhead (a pound-in compression bolt). The buttonhead bolt snapped approximately half an inch into its hole. Inspection of the bolt revealed corrosion below the surface and that the bolt may have been fractured prior to the accident. While most modern

A small rescue team moves an injured climber down steep talus beneath Temple Crag to reach a helicopter landing site. *Julie Vargo / Inyo County SAR*

expansion and glue-in bolts are strong and reliable (when placed correctly in good rock), climbers should be suspicious of any older-style bolts, which are often not drilled deeply. Age greatly affects the integrity of most bolts; this one was likely placed on the first ascent in 1992. The climber could have prevented this accident by implementing some form of redundancy or a true self-belay (utilizing an anchor near the ground) into his rope-solo system. Instead, he put his faith in single points of protection, well off the ground. It's impossible to say if a helmet would have saved Sederstrom after falling from such a height. (*Source: The Editors.*)

FALL ON ROCK | Failure to Test Hold
Sierra Nevada, Temple Crag

On the morning of September 1, we set off to climb the Surgicle, a beautiful yet obscure feature on the Temple Crag buttress. Peter (22) and I (27) were to climb the East Face (II 5.7), while Gabe (27) and my twin brother Brian (27) were going to climb the North Rib (II 5.8). We would meet at the top and then rappel the east face.

After the first two steep pitches, Peter and I pulled onto easier terrain. Just after 3 p.m., I started up the fourth pitch, where the obvious line of the climb disappeared. I traversed left of the anchor and placed my first piece. I was just about to place my third piece when I decided to make one more move to an improved stance. I had both hands on a large block when it shifted. If I had held on, it would have fallen with me. I let go and fell approximately 35 feet to the ledge I had just traversed. The pieces held and the rope came tight. My right ankle was turned grotesquely outward, and there was a terrible pain in my lower back.

Peter, a trained WFR, was able to reach me safely. I was not bleeding heavily, and after some rest the pain became manageable. Recognizing the risks of moving a patient with a back injury, we chose to traverse back to our original anchor. There we would wait for the other group.

Upon hearing echoed cries for help, Gabe and Brian decided to rappel into a gully on their right. They left gear behind for each emergency rappel anchor, and after the first rappel they had to ascend their stuck rope to free it. Once they reached the ground, they quickly realized we were still up on our route. They tried to follow our line, but fatigue and a reduced rack created a dangerous situation. They then tried a seemingly low-fifth-class scramble to the left. This resulted in another retreat and a stuck and cut rope. Frustrated, they returned to the gully right of the North Rib. They gained as much elevation as they could before simul-climbing some 4th class and finally roping up for one pitch of 5th class to the top. There, they began rappelling the face. At about 7 p.m., Gabe and Brian made contact with Peter. Once we were all together, we tied together our two ropes and lowered me two pitches to the ground in one go.

Gabe, also a trained WFR, and I sheltered under emergency blankets while Brian and Peter hiked back to camp; Peter planned to return with supplies and Brian to hike out for help. The next morning, a SAR team arrived by helicopter and the first rescuers reached us just before 11 a.m. As a team of five, they executed a rescue over steep talus, with critical assistance from both Gabe and Peter. For over six hours, the team lowered me to the point where I could load into a helicopter. I was flown to a hospital in Bishop just after sunset. Almost 30 hours after the fall, I was given treatment for a severely broken right ankle and a burst L2 vertebra.

ANALYSIS

Certainly, the traditional lessons associated with this fall are not lost on this climber: the importance of testing blocks before pulling on them, and the necessity to properly evaluate and protect fall lines. However, on this day our biggest lessons came in the form of communication—or lack of communication—between the two teams on the wall. The other team could hear our calls for help but could not understand us, nor did they know where we were. If we had a better means of communication or had better understood each other's climbing routes, they could have reached us much quicker instead of spending four hours trying alternate routes. This wasted time might have had dire consequences if my injuries had been more serious. (*Source: Eric Hengesbaugh.*)

Editor's note: An interview with Eric Hengesbaugh is featured in the Sharp End podcast. Search for "Rescue in the Palisades" at iTunes or Soundcloud.

Two accounts of accidents on the lower slopes of Mt. Whitney (a slip on any icy slope resulting in a head laceration, and loss of control while glissading) can be found at publications.americanalpineclub.org. They serve as important reminders that serious accidents may happen during the non-technical approach or descent from a climb.

COLORADO

FALL ON SNOW | Inadequate Protection
Rocky Mountain National Park, Deep Freeze

On March 31 we began the direct start of Deep Freeze, a rock chimney (M5-6) that finishes on a low-angle snow slope in a broad gully. This leads to a shelf before rambling ice and a final ice pillar (WI5-6). My partner started up the chimney and found good protection before disappearing above some chockstones. I gradually fed out rope until suddenly a loud rumble flew over me and the rope pulled tight. I turned to see my partner on the snow below, partly suspended by the rope, which was wrapped around the right leg.

I immediately escaped the belay, rapped down to my partner, freed the leg from the rope, and set up another anchor to get us down the approach slope (about 100 feet of steep snow) to a wider snow platform where our packs were. My partner said that near the top of the snow gully, a large snow mushroom had collapsed from underneath, which caused the fall. The slide and fall distance likely totaled more than 100 feet.

My partner was in pain but was able to walk slowly with assistance. Unsure of spinal injury, we called for rescue. A climber passed by the area and provided us with additional help. About five hours later, two park rangers arrived. Several more hours passed before the rest of the rescue team arrived and set up a litter to lower my partner down the talus field. Nine hours passed from our first call for rescue until my partner got airlifted. The injuries included concussion, sprains, fractures, spinal injury, lacerations, and abrasions, but my partner was expected to make a good recovery.

ANALYSIS

Two weeks later, I returned with another partner to recover the gear that we had left behind. I found the last pieces of gear my fallen partner had left: a small cam backed up by a nut. It was clear that the cam took all the force of the fall, since it was bent pretty severely. But it held. Reclimbing this pitch, I set up an intermediate belay above the

Rescuers transport an injured ice climber toward a helicopter landing zone on the frozen Loch in Rocky Mountain National Park. The snow gully in which the climber fell 100 feet or more is partially visible in upper right. *NPS Photo*

chimney before starting up the low-angle snow slope. As I climbed, I was hyper-vigilant about looking for additional protection opportunities. Though I spent an inordinate amount of effort looking, even digging in the snow close to the rock, I could not find any reliable protection. One possibility may have been a picket, but this would be unusual gear to carry for a hard ice climb and for Rocky Mountain National Park's winter snow conditions. Another possibility could have been protection way off to the left, halfway up the slope. The only protection I found below the collapsed snow mushroom was a cam in a flared, icy crack–this was definitely "mental" protection.

Alpine climbing is always a balance between speed and risk. We try to move light and fast while mitigating risks. My partner and I are both experienced climbers, and we decided that the low-angle snow slope presented a manageable risk. In this case, we were mistaken. (*Source: Anonymous partner of fallen climber.*)

Editor's note: Two more incidents from northern Colorado in 2015 are documented online. Search "Batman Rock" at publications.americanalpineclub.org for a report of an unroped fall while scouting routes at Lumpy Ridge and "Poudre Canyon" for a serious scrambling fall and rescue.

ROPE DESTRUCTION | Worn Fixed Quickdraw
Boulder Canyon, Coney Island

On September 12, I had a near miss when I was climbing a sport route called Twist and Shout (5.13c) at Coney Island in Boulder Canyon. The route has four fixed

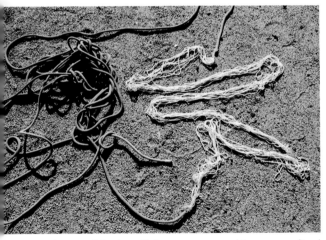

quickdraws on the overhanging top half of the route, two of which are regular quickdraws with a nylon dogbone and two of which are chain-link draws with regular aluminum carabiners on the clipping ends. I briefly looked at the carabiners as I clipped them on my onsight attempt and did not notice any excessive wear or grooving. As I fell above the third fixed draw, which was a chain-link draw with an aluminum carabiner, the biner cut the sheath of the rope, exposing nearly 20 feet of the core.

A rope "de-gloved" by a worn carabiner on a fixed quickdraw in Boulder Canyon. *Jason Haas*

ANALYSIS
While Boulder Canyon is an extremely popular place to climb, this particular route is somewhat obscure and does not see a lot of traffic, so the condition of the fixed gear is not well documented. Instead of going bolt to bolt to inspect the moves and the fixed gear, I was focusing on an onsight attempt and only gave the fixed draws a cursory inspection, because the clips were difficult.

Most of the danger from fixed draws comes from excessive grooving when the carabiner gets worn down. However, carabiners that come in contact with the bolt hanger can get nicks, abrasions, and small, rough teeth that are hard to see without careful inspection. When these carabiners are then placed on the rope-receiving end of the draw, such as for a replacement carabiner on a fixed draw, such burrs can knife the sheath. These can be very difficult to see, especially if you hang directly on the rope running through fixed draws when going bolt to bolt. If the condition of the gear is unknown, it's a good idea to clip directly into the bolt hanger with an independent draw, then fully inspect the fixed draw's condition before committing to using it. (*Source: Jason Haas.*)

Editor's note: Fixed quickdraws must be inspected and replaced frequently. Steel carabiners last much longer than aluminum biners in such uses, but even steel biners eventually can develop rope-damaging grooves, nicks, and burrs.

FALL ON ROCK | Protection Pulled Out
Boulder Canyon, The Boulderado

On March 16, in the early evening, I was climbing at the Boulderado. As a moderately experienced climber, but new trad leader, I attempted to lead Jam It (5.8-). This single-pitch route passes a small roof with a great hand-size crack. After placing a cam vertically in the crack, I pulled up over the roof and bulge to a small shelf. While squatting on this ledge, with one hand gently jammed in the crack, I attempted to place a nut. As I attempted to set the nut, it pulled out. The unexpected jerking motion resulted in enough momentum to pull me off the ledge, resulting in a significant fall of roughly 15 to 20 feet, including slack and rope stretch. I slammed into the wall below the roof on my right flank and hip, coming to a stop about eight to ten feet above the ground.

The impact resulted in significant pain and bruising to my pelvis and right, lower kidney area. X-rays and a CAT scan revealed no fractures or severe internal bleeding, but I did have bruising, abrasions, and lacerations. (*Source: Anonymous report to Accidents website.*)

ANALYSIS
Overconfidence on a relatively flat, wide ledge resulted in a lapse of attention. It's not uncommon for a nut to pull out when you're setting it. Anticipate this possibility and place nuts from solid holds in a well-balanced position. A light tug is usually enough to assure the piece—and the climber—stays put. (*Source: The Editors.*)

FALL ON ROCK | Inadequate Tree Anchor
Boulder Canyon

On August 16, 2014, a guide (uncertified) took four clients (two males and two females in their 20s) to a top-rope climbing area in Boulder Canyon. None of the clients had climbed before.

The clients first did two routes that had anchor bolts with chains at the top. The clients successfully climbed them and were then lowered, being belayed by other clients and the guide.

To set up the third top-rope, the guide used a single anchor: a sling tied around a tree less than six inches in diameter, with a shallow root system. One client successfully climbed the route and was lowered. Another client did the climb and was also lowered to the ground. This same client then tried again, reached the top, and began downclimbing. He was about about 30 feet from the ground when he fell. The guide was belaying him, but the tree came loose and the client (and the tree) fell to the ground.

The climber's helmet was cracked and bloody, but he was conscious and wanted to get up. After a call to 911, Boulder County sheriff's deputies arrived in 15 minutes, followed by an ambulance. The injured climber was transported to the hospital, where he was diagnosed with a broken wrist, shattered ribs, and a concussion. His recovery took over a year, and he still suffers some memory loss.

ANALYSIS
Local climbers indicated that they did not use this particular tree as an anchor because of its small diameter, shallow root system, and dry, shallow soil on top of the cliff. The guide was reported to have said that a living tree is OK if it is over three inches in diameter. A minimum of five or six inches is the accepted standard. A very healthy, well-rooted three-inch tree might be considered, but only as a redundant anchor point. The clients and other climbers nearby pointed out that the guide did not test the anchor. (*Source: Jed Williamson, from local reports and interview with the injured climber.*)

STRANDED | Climbing Alone
Boulder, Second Flatiron

On March 6 a solo climber attempted Call the Copps, an ephemeral ice climb (WI3 M3) on the east face of the Second Flatiron. When he found the route deteriorating in warm weather and threatened by falling ice, he instead climbed mixed terrain near the most popular rock route up the face (5.0) until he reached a point where he felt he couldn't climb up or down. Fearing a fall, he called for help and Rocky Mountain Rescue assisted his escape from the face. (*Source: News articles and first-person report at MountainProject.com.*)

ANALYSIS
Although the climber started fairly early (he called for help around 9 a.m.), conditions change rapidly on these sunny faces. The ability to judge conditions and willingness to turn around—integral to successful alpine climbing—apply no less on "practice climbs" within shouting distance of a small city. (*Source: The Editors.*)

Editor's note: Two other incidents in the Flatirons in 2015 are reported online: Search "Gregory Flatironette" at publications.americanalpineclub.org for a fatality involving a solo climber and "Angels Way" for a serious fall during the approach to Skunk Canyon.

STRANDED | Late Start, Darkness, Failed to Follow Directions
Eldorado Canyon, Redgarden Wall

My climbing partner and I (ages 33 and 30) arrived at Eldo early on March 29, intending to climb Swanson's Arête, a multi-pitch 5.5. We got to the base around 10

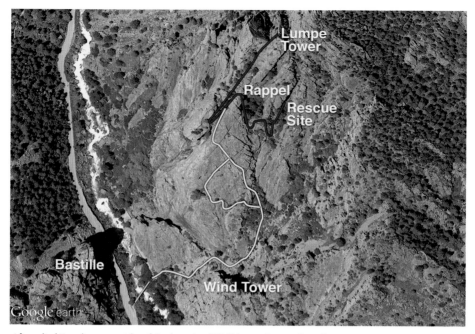

After climbing the west side of Redgarden Wall (top of image) and topping out on Lumpe Tower at sunset, two climbers who had never done the complex East Slabs descent got lost (red line) and called for a rescue at 11:30 p.m. The standard descent options (approximate) are in yellow.

a.m. There was a very inexperienced party starting the first pitch of an adjacent route when we arrived. They were knocking down lots of rocks, so we waited for them before starting up the West Chimney approach pitch. My partner led the first pitch, and then a free soloist asked me if he could climb through, which I allowed. Due to all these delays, we were not both on the ledge from which the actual route starts until sometime after noon.

I had climbed other 5.5 routes in Eldorado Canyon, but Swanson's Arête felt significantly more difficult, which led to delays. We made it to the summit of Lumpe Tower around 7 p.m. In late March the sun was just beginning to dip behind the mountains, and the impending darkness created a sense of urgency. We reached a notch below the summit block and discussed our options. My partner had seen another party get ropes stuck on the Dirty Deeds rappel route, the closest descent path, earlier in the day. Because we had left the car so early in the day, I had not brought a headlamp, and we decided to avoid the Dirty Deeds rappel out of concern about getting a rope stuck with only one headlamp between us.

We decided to follow a mostly easy gully off the back of the peak. We assumed we would find the standard East Slabs descent from Redgarden Wall, and that we could belay each other if a downclimb looked questionable. (Editor's note: The East Slabs descent route is difficult to follow the first time one does it, even in daylight, and has extensive and exposed 3rd- and 4th-class downclimbing.) The gully took us to a clearing, and by this point it was night. We found cairns and continued to walk downhill until we cliffed out. We walked back up to the clearing and assessed our options. Two other directions cliffed out. The remaining side had a cairn that led us to a number of slings tied around a constriction, with rappel rings. We assumed this was a proper descent and made the rappel.

The mystery rappel placed us into a fairly flat, heavily vegetated area with steep walls on three sides. We explored this area in every direction and eventually skirted an exposed walkway to a similar but larger area. We continued downhill until finding extremely dense brush. In the dark of night, we could not tell if the brush was hiding a cliff. After exhausting all other directions, we settled into an open section, back uphill, and admitted that we were completely lost. We called for a rescue sometime around 11:30 p.m., giving GPS coordinates from our phone.

The search and rescue team arrived impressively quickly, told us we were in a "no man's land" section of Eldorado, and guided us through the descent, which involved some bushwhacking, a lower, a long rappel, more hiking, and a short rappel.

ANALYSIS

This incident was clearly the result of poor decision-making. First, I should not have left my headlamp behind. While lack of light was never an issue (the moon was bright, and we had one headlamp and cell phone lights), the fact that I did not carry my headlamp contributed to the decisions we made.

Second, when we were at the top of the second pitch, we realized we were behind on time. At this point we should have considered calling it a day and descending.

We made our biggest mistake upon reaching the summit. The guidebook listed three descent options, but made all of them sound tricky. We blindly followed the path of least resistance, assuming it would take us to the East Slabs.

We did do some things right. We both had down jackets and plenty of water. We were not in imminent danger. We also brought walkie-talkies, which made communicating with SAR easy once they arrived in the area. We were able to contact SAR and send them our exact location because we had a cell phone with us. (Despite seeing our location on Google Maps, we could not glean any useful information to aid in our descent.) Many online critics have second-guessed our decision to call SAR, but I still believe this was the right choice. I've always read that the best thing to do when you're lost in the backcountry is to stay put and wait for help. That's what we did. Had we continued to search for a way down on questionable terrain, it may have lead to a real accident with serious consequences. (*Source: Anonymous report from one of the climbers.*)

FALL ON ROCK | Inadequate Protection
Eldorado Canyon, Bastille Crack

On the morning of July 13, a party was climbing the first pitch of the Bastille Crack (5.7+), which was well within the leader's climbing ability. The leader placed his first piece in a crack/flake about nine feet off the deck, then climbed up a couple of feet and began moving into the crack to the left (a move usually considered the crux of the climb). Here the leader placed a second piece, a 0.75 Camalot, about four feet above and three feet left of the first piece. About eight feet above the second piece, the leader's foot popped and he fell. During the fall the leader became inverted and, according to the belayer, struck headfirst on the corner of a flake toward the end of the fall. Both climbers were wearing helmets. The belayer noticed blood coming from the leader's head and called to him with no response.

The belayer lowered the inverted leader four feet to the ground, by which time he was conscious and able to right himself and sit. The second (a physician's assistant) removed the leader's helmet and noticed a significant cut at the left temple. The second began basic first aid, and once the leader was able to move, the party went to the emergency department, where four stitches were placed. The leader's helmet had significant damage, including a crack, a deep indentation, and discoloration throughout the left side.

ANALYSIS

The climbers felt there were two causes of the fall leading to the injury. The primary one was that the leader (with 13 years' climbing experience) took for granted the relatively easy route and his familiarity with it, and did not place adequate gear. While normally living by the mantra of "place early and often," in this case the leader had climbed well above his last piece, putting him at risk of striking flakes near the ground.

The secondary cause (also due to the party taking the route for granted) was the position of the belayer, who was standing approximately eight feet from the wall and was not tethered in any way. The belayer weighed about 50 pounds less than leader, and when the fall occurred the belayer was pulled into the wall and upward, adding probably eight to ten feet to the fall. (*Source: Anonymous online submission by the leader.*)

FALL ON ROCK | Lowering Error, Inadequate Belay
Eldorado Canyon, The Naked Edge

Two experienced climbers, ages 31 and 28, were attempting the Naked Edge (5.11b) in August. The leader of the 5.11a first pitch belayed at a two-bolt anchor and set up to belay the second directly off the anchor with an ATC-Guide device in autoblock mode. After the second took tension to retrieve a stuck cam, he asked to be lowered a few feet before starting to climb again. The leader threaded a sling through the "release hole" of the device and redirected the sling through a carabiner clipped to one of the anchor bolts, so he could release

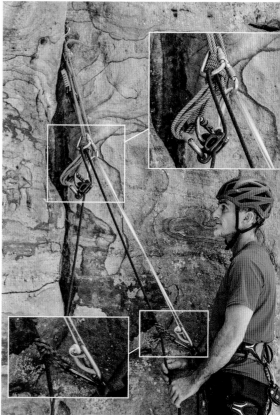

One method for backing up a lower from a direct belay with an autoblocking device. The weighted rope is redirected through the belay anchor and then backed up with a friction hitch clipped to the belayer's harness. *Sterling Snyder*

the device and lower the second. In an email to *Rock and Ice* magazine, the climber said, "It took a lot of pull to get the ATC-Guide to release, but when it did, my partner [started falling]. I grabbed the brake side of the rope, but that didn't help. I just got burns on my hand.... My partner stopped when he hit the ledge. I don't think the belay system did much other than slow him down." The second climber was lucky to escape with a minor concussion, abrasions, and bruised heels. (*Source: Rock and Ice magazine.*)

ANALYSIS

It is very difficult to control the speed when releasing an autoblocking belay device to lower in this fashion. As the manufacturer recommends, the belay must be backed up when the device is used in autoblock (guide) mode to lower a climber. This can be done either with a friction hitch connecting the belayer to the "up" rope (brake-hand side) running through the redirect (*as shown in the illustration on the previous page*) or by using a Munter hitch or a second belay device to belay the "up" rope off the belayer's harness with one hand, while releasing the autoblock with the other hand and/or body weight.

These techniques should not be learned on the fly. Practice them with real-world loads and full backup before relying on them to lower a climber. (*Source: The Editors.*)

LOWERING ERROR | Inexperience, Communication Issues
Pikes Peak

On August 22 a female climber (age 39) was injured while being lowered from the anchor after top-roping a trad climb. She was in a climbing party of five exploring a granite crag near the Crags Trailhead. Just below the anchor, it was necessary to lower over a large overlap to reach the slab below. As she pushed off the lip, the climber free-fell to the slab, approximately eight feet down, fracturing the calcaneus and talus bones in her heel and ankle. The climber and belayer (age 29) had met through an online post and had not climbed together before the day of the incident. (*Source: Mountain Project.*)

ANALYSIS

This incident was discussed at length on a Mountain Project forum. The parties involved disagreed about the causes and conclusions. The analysis below outlines general actions that can be taken by climbers and belayers to avoid this type of incident.

In this particular incident, the source of slack in the system cannot be determined definitively, and likely resulted from a combination of factors. Slabs and other rock features can create friction in the system that make it difficult to feel the weight of the lowering climber (or can disguise the fact that the climber has unweighted the system). Before lowering over the lip in this incident, the climber expressed that she hesitated, a pause that the belayer stated he did not feel and may have caused slack to be added. While lowering, the rope can shift over features, suddenly creating slack. When lowering from a slab (little weight on the rope) to vertical or overhanging rock, some rope stretch should be anticipated, and a pendulum swing may also result. For all of these reasons, a belayer should anticipate sudden additional force while lowering over a roof, overlap, or corner, or anytime the climber is out of view. If the climber unweights the rope by standing or grabbing the rock, the belayer should take out any slack in the system and sit in the harness until the climber communicates that he or she is ready to continue lowering. This minimizes rope stretch once lowering recommences.

The climber should clearly and loudly communicate with the belayer anytime he or she unweights the rope or needs to maneuver around an obstacle. Once the climber is ready to resume lowering, a hard "take" should be requested to eliminate any stretch or slack that could be introduced into the system. On lower-angle or vertical terrain, when the belayer is out of view, consider a rappel descent instead of lowering.

Prior to climbing, the belayer and climber should discuss the climb and the descent to understand the particular risks of the route and to communicate preferences. This is especially important when climbing with new partners or strangers. (*Source: The Editors.*)

LOWERING ERROR | Inexperience, Communication
Turkey Rocks, Turkey Perch

On February 7, a female climber with two years of climbing experience executed a slow but clean lead of Left Handed Jew, a 5.7 trad route. I was top-rope belaying a climber 20 feet to the left of their route. During the climb, several observers noted that verbal communication between the lead climber and her belayer (the climber's boyfriend, also with two years of experience) was mildly problematic, requiring repeated back and forth exchanges to clarify communication. When she reached the top of the climb, the leader set up a gear anchor.

At this point, the climber and belayer began discussing a descent/lowering plan for the first time. The leader and belayer were not in visual contact, due to the rounded, sloping terrain at the top of the route. The belayer suggested that he "just climb it," so that they could get down and eat lunch. I correctly inferred his intention to be that she pull up the rope and give him a belay from the top of the route, followed by a short walk-off. This, however, was not understood by the leader. The belayer took the leader off and called "off belay." A moment later, we heard a crashing sound and looked to see

A climber leads the route Left Handed Jew at Turkey Perch. *Dougald MacDonald*

the climber rapidly tumbling down the wall. We shouted for the belayer to stop the fall, and he managed to grab the rope bare-handed, arresting the climber 15 feet from the ground.

The belayer was unable to lower the climber further due to a very high amount of rope drag. I lowered my climber to the ground, climbed up to the injured climber, and pulled her down by body-weighting her harness.

The response from the climbers at the crag was composed and effective, with approximately a dozen climbers organizing to aid the victim, several with wilderness first responder training. The climber was neurologically intact, denied impacting her head (she was not wearing a helmet), and was found to have a small, bleeding puncture wound on her buttocks. She reported pain in the arm, back and the sacrum. Though able to walk unassisted briefly, persistent lightheadedness resulted in the decision by local fire department personnel to evacuate by helicopter. The injured climber was later diagnosed with a fractured sacrum. (*Source: Mark Williams, R.N.*)

ANALYSIS

This incident could have been avoided easily by discussing the climb and descent options and agreeing on a plan before the climber left the ground. When communication is difficult, simple climbing commands and using each other's names will reduce confusion. Before lowering, ensure that you are on belay before removing your direct connection to the anchors. Have your belayer pull out any slack in the system so it is obvious he or she is holding your weight. Friction in the system might make it difficult to know that you are on belay, so you can control the descent by grabbing the rope that runs between the belayer and the anchors, and feeding it through the anchors until the belay is visually confirmed.

In this incident, the belayer was able to arrest the fall by bare-handing the rope without burning his hands even slightly. I later seconded the route on their rope in order to clean their gear. I cleaned a total of 17 cams on a 70-foot route with less than ideal use of extensions. The amount of rope drag was truly unusual for such a short climb, but likely prevented a ground fall. (*Sources: Mark Williams and the Editors.*)

FALL ON ROCK | Climbing Unroped
Sangre de Cristo Range, Crestone Needle

On September 3, Dr. Matt Davis (41), a trauma director at Scott & Baylor Memorial Hospital in Temple, Texas, and his partner, Ryan Brown, attempted Crestone Needle, a 14,203-foot peak, via the Ellingwood Arête (III 5.7). Davis and Brown selected the route's direct start, climbing three pitches of 5.6/5.7, instead of a longer 3rd-class traverse on ledges to reach the upper pitches. Davis and Brown had completed the initial roped section and were scrambling 3rd-class ledges toward the final pitches when Davis slipped, falling over 100 feet to a large ledge system above the lower wall. Brown descended to his partner and discovered that he had died upon impact. (*Source: Rock and Ice and Custer County Search and Rescue.*)

ANALYSIS

It is not uncommon to encounter a mix of 5th-class climbing and scrambles during a mountain ascent, but the risks of climbing unroped must be weighed and quick belays considered. According to Cindy Howard of Custer County Search and Rescue (CCSAR), the fall may have been partially attributed to Davis wearing climbing shoes during the scrambling section. While climbing shoes are appropriate for fifth-class rock, the smooth rubber can be slick on muddy, icy, snowy, or grass-covered surfaces, and great care must be taken when scrambling in rock shoes. Approach shoes may have been more appropriate for this section of the climb. (*Sources: Cindy Howard, CCSAR Captain, and the Editors.*)

FALLS ON SNOW AND ROCK | Inadequate Gear
Sangre de Cristo Range, Crestone Peak

Several accidents, including one fatality, occurred in the Red Gully on the standard route up 14,294-foot Crestone Peak. Although it faces south, this rocky gully often holds snow well into July, presenting mountaineering challenges on what is otherwise a 3rd-class scramble.

The Ellingwood Arête of Crestone Needle climbs the blunt prow facing the camera. The Red Gully on Crestone Peak (peak on far right) lies on the opposite side.

On Saturday, July 11, Jennifer Staufer (39) and her climbing partner, Adam Vonnahme (38), climbed Crestone via the south face (class III). Both climbers had multiple 14er summits; Crestone was Jennifer's 41st 14er. While ascending, they wore Micro Spikes and used ice axes, due to ice and snow on the route. During the descent, the snow appeared to be soft enough to forgo the Micro spikes. Near 13,000 feet, Jennifer slipped on an icy patch while crossing a couloir. Unable to self-arrest, she fell approximately 150 feet, stopping in a snowmelt waterfall. She had to wait for her climbing partner to help her move or she might have fallen farther.

Adam used both his cell phone and SPOT device to request help, texting important patient information, including that his partner was 10 weeks pregnant, likely had multiple fractures (including rib fractures and a broken leg), was cold and wet, and was having difficulty breathing. Saguache County SAR (SAGSAR), Custer County SAR (CCSAR), and Western Mountain Rescue Team (WMRT) of Gunnison County responded to the incident.

A Blackhawk helicopter from the High Altitude Army Aviation Site (HAATS) was in the area on another SAR mission on Blanca Peak. After completing that mission and refueling, seven CCSAR climbers were transported to the Cottonwood drainage at approximately 6 p.m. The helicopter then transported five members of WMRT to the scene, and EagleMed Salida inserted two SAGSAR personnel, for a total of 14 field personnel. Conditions in the couloir included wet rock, running water, snow, and ice.

The patient was stabilized and then lowered in a Stokes litter, in difficult terrain and in darkness, to a landing zone in the Cottonwood Basin, from which she was airlifted to Crestone at 1 a.m. She was transferred to the hospital for treatment of several serious injuries, including a closed pneumothorax (collapsed lung).

On Sunday afternoon, at 2 p.m., CCSAR was again activated, this time to assist Anika Jimenez (23), who also fell in the Red Gully on Crestone Peak and had an ankle injury. With a splinted ankle, she was able to hike out to the South Colony Lakes Trail, below Broken Hand Pass, where CCSAR members transferred her out of the basin via a Stokes litter. Earlier that morning, CCSAR members had encountered Jimenez's party during the descent from the Staufer incident. They told the party of the earlier incident and warned them of conditions in the couloir.

On July 24, less than two weeks later, Christopher Kiryluk (34) died from a fall in the Red Gully. Similar to the incidents on July 11 and 12, the climber was not wearing crampons or Micro Spikes, and he slipped and fell on the descent.

On August 14, Bruce Owen (age unknown) suffered a broken ankle from a slip and fall in the same descent route. Two CCSAR members responded, assisted the subject to a landing zone, and bivied until dawn, when Flight For Life could land to transport the patient to an area hospital.

ANALYSIS

These accidents highlight the importance of being adequately equipped for a variety of conditions—and utilizing the equipment you carry—on the more difficult 14er climbs. Standard route descriptions may not warn climbers of early season snowpack, melting snow, and the associated increase in danger from falling ice and rock. These conditions often make climbs in the Crestones technical. Peakbaggers need to ascertain the conditions and turn back when they exceed their equipment or ability. (*Source: Cindy Howard, Custer County Search and Rescue Captain.*)

FALL ON ROCK | Poor Position, No Helmet, Inexperience
Summit County, White Cliff

On June 7 a woman (29) suffered a serious head injury while leading a 5.9 sport route. After clipping the first quickdraw (previously placed by her belayer, age 26), the climber slipped before clipping the second draw. The belayer did not remember seeing the rope behind the climber's leg, but once tension came on the rope the climber flipped upside-down, violently hit her head against the wall, and lost consciousness. The belayer lowered her to the ground and called 911. She was unresponsive for approximately three minutes.

Two Summit County Rescue Group members (both EMTs), along with a Wildland Fire Unit (an EMT and a paramedic), were in the vicinity and responded to the call, reaching the party and beginning treatment within 20 minutes of the accident. Within another 10 to 15 minutes, an additional paramedic and other rescuers with medical and extrication resources joined the first responders. The patient had an open skull fracture. She was loaded into a litter and evacuated along the steep, loose trail, requiring three separate belays. She was then transported to Summit Medical Center by ambulance and ultimately was flown to Denver by a Flight for Life helicopter.

ANALYSIS

The primary cause of the injury was the climber allowing the rope to get behind her leg, which easily can flip a climber upside-down in a leader fall. It is important to keep the lead rope in front of your feet and legs whenever possible. While the climber had three years of climbing experience, she was not an experienced lead climber (fewer than 25 total leads).

The severity of the head injury likely would have been reduced if the climber had been wearing a helmet. Both the climber and the more experienced belayer did not regularly wear helmets while climbing, and the belayer stated that he understood them only to be useful in protecting against rockfall. While helmets are primarily designed to protect heads from falling objects, they also can help prevent skull fractures and lacerations during leader falls. (*Source: Summit County Rescue Group.*)

FALL ON ROCK | Inadequate Protection
Black Canyon of the Gunnison National Park

I (32 at the time, with 20 years of experience) broke my ankle in a lead fall in the Black Canyon of the Gunnison as the moon rose on September 25. I had been a bit cavalier when Jack Cody (age 30) and I rappelled off the south rim at sunrise to climb Astro Dog (V 5.11d) in a day. Jack and I had climbed enough routes in the Black that we felt very comfortable on its committing walls, where the only way home is to climb out. Astro Dog was supposed to be the warm-up route on a four-day trip.

It was dark by the time I started pitch ten—the crux. We knew we would be finishing by headlamp, but I'd hoped to have daylight for onsighting the glass-smooth stem corner. In spite of the darkness, I was certain I could hike the slippery moves, even with a backpack and tagline.

The crux boulder problem starts off a small ledge. I placed a bomber yellow Alien at waist-height from the ledge. However, I couldn't find solid gear that would keep me off the ledge if I fell. I placed a marginal brass nut in a shallow, flaring pin scar and pulled into a desperate layback. I was two inches from a fingerlock, with the brass nut at my waist, when I slipped. The nut popped, I fell about six feet, and I clipped the ledge with my right foot as the rope came tight. I sat on the ledge and rubbed my ankle. I'd shattered my talus bone and ripped some cartilage, but I didn't know that yet. I convinced myself it was a sprain. While catching my breath, I noticed some handholds behind me that I hadn't seen before and decided to try again.

This time I did what I should have done the first time: I stood in a sling from the yellow Alien at my waist and placed a micro-cam (number 00 C3 Camalot) that would keep me off the ledge. With good preclipped gear, I stepped back down to the ledge and fired the crux 30 feet to the top of the dihedral, where my ankle gave out for good. I was cross-stepping onto a slab when my foot turned into a noodle. No matter how much I willed my right foot to take weight, it just flopped to the side. I was 10 feet above my last gear and realized how foolish it would be to continue on one leg. I downclimbed and dropped onto the rope.

Jack took over the lead. I finished the climb (several more pitches) by using my knee and grabbing gear whenever possible. Prusiking would have been more difficult and time-consuming because of the zigzag character of the pitches. When Jack finished the last pitch at 1 a.m., he tied off the rope and went to the truck parked nearby. He got jumars and aiders and lowered them down to me to spare me the effort of thrashing up a loose 5.9 chimney.

ANALYSIS

In retrospect, my overconfidence and hastiness were the main factors leading to the accident. I wish I'd taken a few extra minutes to evaluate the crux before launching into it. There is a tendency to feel rushed when darkness falls. However, it was already dark and the weather was stable—there was no real reason to rush. If I'd taken the extra time, I probably would have seen the proper sequence and maybe not have fallen at all. Also, my pride clouded my judgment. If I had stood in a sling and preplaced the micro-cam before the first try, I probably would not have hit the ledge.

We also made some good decisions that kept me safe overall: I picked an extremely reliable partner (Jack is an AMGA certified rock guide and solid 5.12 climber); we had headlamps and plenty of clothing, food and water; and the forecast was ideal. After the accident, we moved slowly and carefully, wary of our fatigue and the fact that we were in a bad position if Jack got hurt. Thankfully, because of all these good decisions, getting out with a broken ankle was more of a mini-adventure than a rescue. (*Source: Derek Franz.*)

FALL ON ROCK | Belay Error, Communication Problems
Black Canyon of the Gunnison National Park

On October 24, Daniel Fullmer (34, over 15 years of experience) and I (32 years old, 15 years of experience) were climbing Scenic Cruise (V 5.10d). There was a party above us and at least another party within earshot on a nearby route. I was leading the Pegmatite Traverse (5.9+, pitch six). I was eight to ten feet shy of the anchor when I took an unexpected fall. I fell approximately 20 feet, hit a slabby ledge, flipped upside-down, and continued falling another 30 to 40 feet until the rope went taut. I had lost both my climbing shoes in the fall. I did a quick body scan and found I had minor scrapes on my ankles and left shoulder, a mild headache, and strong pain in my right ribs. I did not lose consciousness or feel lightheaded; my alertness was sufficient and I had no pain in my neck or back.

I began to yell to Daniel to let him know I was OK, but I did not hear a response. I tied a prusik around the rope, inserted the rope in my Grigri, and began to ascend. I jugged up about 20 feet to a ledge where I found an old 1/4-inch bolt, and clipped in. I put on my approach shoes and tried again to establish communication with Daniel, with no response. My ribs were really hurting, and with every extension it felt like they were on fire. Just as I began to ascend toward a higher ledge, I noticed movement in the rope and assumed Daniel was moving toward me.

I could see my gear at this point—a 0.75 BD Camelot had popped (marginal placement), but the rest of the gear had held. The failed piece had only added about five to eight feet to my fall. The last piece of gear, a yellow Metolius TCU, was bomber, but I did not want both of us weighting the piece, so I waited at the ledge for Daniel. He ascended to a big ledge, built an anchor, and lowered to me. We decided that we needed to bail, as I had lost my climbing shoes and was worried that I'd fractured my ribs. We proceeded to rappel the Cruise route, doing a total of five rappels.

A climber leads the infamous Pegmatite Traverse on the Scenic Cruise. *Jediah Porter*

We ended up losing a few cams, nuts, and webbing, but overall we got down quickly and efficiently. I ended up with a several muscle tears, a mild concussion, and bruised ribs, but no fractures or lasting injuries. My new Black Diamond Vapor helmet took the majority of the blow, with an indentation the size of a softball about 3/8-inch deep in the right rear and bottom of the helmet. I'm lucky I was wearing this new helmet, as my old-school suspension helmet does not cover the full back of my head.

ANALYSIS

After debriefing the incident, I discovered that Daniel had clearly heard the command, "Daniel, off belay." Whether there was another climber named Daniel in a neighboring party or he had just misunderstood a nearby "off belay" command, he believed it was me who had shouted and took me off belay. I fell shortly afterward.

I had experienced something similar while belaying on the previous pitch, hearing some faint command, but I decided to keep the belay on, thinking that I would remove it once the rope was being pulled in rapidly, indicating Daniel was preparing to belay me. About five minutes later, I heard a clear, "Chas, off belay," confirming that the original, faint command had not been from Daniel. The brain unquestionably hears what it expects to hear.

In such a situation, when there is environmental noise, the climber is out of sight of the belayer, or other climbers are nearby, using names with shouted belay commands is essential, as is waiting for confirmation before taking a climber off belay or unclipping from an anchor. When communication is completely lost, the belayer should wait until all slack has been pulled up before taking the leader off belay. (*Source: Chas Robles.*)

RAPPEL ERROR | Hair Caught In Rappel Device
Vallecito, Lemon Reservoir

It was a beautiful morning on Memorial Day weekend. We had the best spot to camp for the Lemon Reservoir crag. One party already had passed our camp, heading into the canyon to the routes. Our group was just finishing scarfing down our bacon and eggs when we heard a female cry of sheer pain. We immediately took off in a dead sprint to the bottom of the routes.

Upon getting to the routes, we could see a girl (mid-20s) dangling from her hair in her ATC (she was rappelling a route). I sprinted back to camp to grab another rope and my harness. When I got to the top of the cliff, her partner had already rigged a rappel and lowered to assist. He put a prusik above her ATC and attached a sling. The woman was able to stand in the sling, releasing her hair from the ATC. Her helmet was dangling from her harness the whole time. When we returned to our camp, we could think of nothing more than the fact that if the helmet had been worn the hair could have been contained to the back of the head and out of the way. This may not be a brain buster, but helmets matter! (*Source: Dillon Parker.*)

ANALYSIS
While a helmet may have helped keep the hair away from the device in this case, it does not ensure the hair is contained, especially for climbers with long hair. Keeping hair secured in a braid or bun, at the back of the head, is the best way to reduce the risk of it being pulled into the device by the rope while belaying or rappelling. Fortunately for this woman, the top of the route was accessible by foot and several climbers at the crag were proficient in rescue techniques. (*Source: The Editors.*)

FALL ON ICE | Climbing Unroped
Eureka, First Gully

On January 30, Mark Miller (50) took a fatal fall while guiding First Gully, a four-pitch WI3 ice climb near Eureka. Miller, a climbing guide from Ouray, and his two clients were nearing the top of the low-angle climb. Miller was free soloing alongside the clients, giving pointers as one led the pitch, when he fell. According to the clients, a bulge of ice fractured unexpectedly under Miller and carried him down the route, about 800 feet. After descending, the climbers (one of whom was an emergency-room doctor) confirmed that Miller had died from injuries sustained in the fall. (*Sources: Rock and Ice magazine, Climbing magazine.*)

ANALYSIS
Miller was an influential member of the climbing community and an accomplished climber, with over 20 years of guiding experience. Even though First Gully was well within his soloing abilities, ice conditions are never certain. By climbing alongside his client, it is possible that Miller was forced out of the optimal line on the route and onto less solid ice. Fall protection should be considered whenever the consequences are major, even if the likelihood of a fall is very small. (*Source: The Editors.*)

GEORGIA

RAPPEL ERROR
Pigeon Mountain, Rocktown

Suzanne Huffman (40) was climbing with a church group on October 10. While rappelling, she fell 30 feet to the ground and died from her injuries. One of her sons, who witnessed the accident, told reporters, "She was getting ready to go down and the device was clipped into the rope, and it was unhinged just enough for the rope to slip out." (*Source: News reports.*)

ANALYSIS
Although it's unknown what caused this climber to become detached from her rappel ropes, the incident is a reminder of the importance of a safety check before every rappel. Both you and your partners should double-check the anchor, make sure both ends of the rope(s) reach their intended destination, be sure the rappel device is set up correctly and the rappel carabiner's gate is locked, and assess the need for a backup and/or blocking knots in the rope ends. (*Source: The Editors.*)

IDAHO

FALL ON ROCK | Inadequate Protection
Sawtooth Mountains, Elephants Perch

On July 7, Anna Dvorak, 28, died as a result of injuries from a long leader fall on the third pitch of the Mountaineers Route (III 5.9). Dvorak's climbing partner had led the first pitch, linking the usual pitch one and most of pitch two into a long lead. She took the lead for the next pitch, passing the normal anchor for pitch two and continuing up the 5.8 third pitch. Somewhere above the mid-pitch traverse to the left, out of sight from her belayer, Dvorak took a long, swinging, inverted fall. She was wearing a helmet but nonetheless suffered a serious head injury.

Two other people heard calls for help and climbed to the second-pitch belay ledge on the route, where they gave first aid to the patient. However, she soon lost vital

Elephants Perch. Red dot marks the approximate location of the fall on Mountaineers Route. *Steph Abegg*

signs, and after 45 minutes of CPR the climbers gave up trying to resuscitate her. A large, multi-unit rescue team that had already responded to the scene assisted the climbers, then bivouacked near the base of the route and recovered the body the next day. (*Sources: Published eyewitness and SAR reports.*)

ANALYSIS

According to her climbing partner, none of Dvorak's protection pulled out during her fall, which suggests she had not placed enough pro to adequately safeguard the pitch. It's often tempting, especially on longer routes where speed is important, to run it out on terrain that feels easy for you. But placing a few "just in case" pieces can dramatically reduce the consequences of a sudden slip.

Many climbers mistakenly believe that a swinging fall will be slower or have less impact than a straight-down fall; in fact, a pendulum generates just as much speed and impact, and it often increases the chances of hitting an obstacle. Protecting soon after a traverse can mitigate this possibility. In this case, a swing may have contributed to inverting the climber into a headfirst plunge, with disastrous results. (*Source: The Editors.*)

KENTUCKY

FALL ON ROCK | Unable to Clip Anchors, Inadequate Belay
Red River Gorge, Drive-By Crag

During the early afternoon on October 17, some friends and I were climbing at Drive-By Crag. My friends didn't have much outdoor climbing experience. Over a couple of days, I had been watching Jake belay his partner, and I felt confident that he paid attention and was managing the rope appropriately.

I had attempted to lead Breakfast Burrito (5.10d) on an earlier visit. With this knowledge, I made it past my original high point, clipped the last draw before the chains, and shook out before finishing. I couldn't get into a good position to clip the chains, and I spent a fairly long time on a somewhat bad hold and began to tire. I was about four feet from the chains and began to evaluate whether I should try to clip or if I should take the fall. I opted for the fall, yelled "Falling!" and making sure my feet were clear from the rope.

Instead of falling cleanly, I slammed into the rock knee-first, fracturing my left kneecap. I was lowered to the ground, where climbers assisted me and an ER nurse monitored my condition. I was carried out to our vehicle and driven to the ER in Irvine. A few days later, I saw an orthopedic surgeon who decided on a surgery that would repair my patellar tendon and remove bone fragments.

ANALYSIS

According to the others, Jake took in slack and braced himself for a hard catch. He is about 45 pounds heavier than me, and he said he never left the ground while catching my fall. If Jake had adequate slack in the system, or had jumped into the fall, my injury may have been avoided. I spoke with him after the accident, and he noted that he was unfamiliar with the concept of a "soft catch." He stated that he thought the belayer was automatically pulled into the air, because whenever he falls on lead his partner gets pulled up. Additionally, when he belayed his partner, she would yell at him to keep the rope tight. I realize now that when I was watching Jake to evaluate his belaying abilities, I never watched him catch a fall. Whenever he was lead belaying on our trip, everyone was climbing easier climbs well below their abilities. I shouldn't have made assumptions about what my partner knew and didn't know. (*Source: Grant Warman.*)

Editor's note: Accidents 2015 reported a similar incident in Colorado, also resulting in a fractured patella. The appropriate amount of slack in the belay system varies with the climb—too little and a falling climber can be pulled hard into the rock; too much and the climber might fall too far and hit a ledge or other obstacle. As a general rule, when sport climbing, it's appropriate for the belayer to maintain a small arc of slack in the rope and allow his or her body to move and absorb some of the impact of the fall. See "Know the Ropes: Belaying" in this edition for more on this subject.

MONTANA

FALL ON SNOW | Inadequate Equipment
Glacier National Park, Lithoid Cusp

On June 27, experienced mountaineers Jack Beard (60) and David Steele (27) attempted a new route to the Lithoid Cusp, a dramatic spire atop the large east-facing wall between Ipasha Peak and Mt. Merritt. Their route involved much scrambling to reach a steep snow couloir that led another 800 feet to the ridgeline. The two continued unroped up the snow, using ice axes and crampons. At 11:30 a.m., about halfway up the couloir, Beard slipped in the soft snow and slid to the bottom of the couloir, continuing over rocks and a cascade of snowmelt until he came to a stop on a small outcropping after sliding about 600 feet.

Steele climbed down to his partner, who had fractures in his ribs, spine, and right forearm, as well as a concussion. He built a platform where Beard could rest, anchored him, marked the area with a high-visibility yellow tent, and prepared Beard to spend the night. At 2 p.m., he left for help, reclimbing the snow couloir to the ridge and then descending the far

The red line shows a new route attempted by two climbers in Glacier National Park. (1) Site of the fall. (2) Point where climber stopped falling (600 feet lower) and was later rescued. *David Steele* side toward Mokowanis Lake. At 5:45 p.m. he found a hiker with an InReach satellite communication device who was able to send a message requesting help. Steele arranged to meet a ranger who would hike in his direction, and they connected at 8:15 p.m. Rangers called for a helicopter rescue. A Two Bear Air Rescue helicopter lowered a crew member to Beard's ledge, picked him up, and transported him to the valley and an ambulance.

ANALYSIS

By email, Steele described the climbers' decision-making before and during this incident: "In the wake of the accident, both Jack and I spent a bunch of time talking and considering what we could have done differently. The trip placed diverse needs on our gear and ourselves: overnight gear, a complete alpine rack, two ropes, food and fuel, plus snow climbing equipment. We went about as light as we felt comfortable, which meant crampons and one ice tool each. We agree that two tools would have been more secure and could have prevented Jack's slip. His ice tool was especially compact—it worked well for piton use, but that meant it wasn't suited to self arrest. An axe with a more alpine-style pick and longer handle would have been a better choice.

"Unseasonably hot weather at the time of the accident meant that the snow surface wasn't even close to refreezing at night; it's unlikely that an earlier start would have yielded more consolidated snow. Protection in the rock along the snow couloir was poor at best, and we elected not to carry a stack of pickets to make running protection. Because we couldn't protect the climb, our opinion was that roping together just endangered both climbers. We elected to solo both the rock and the snow based on our comfort levels.

"It's worth mentioning that Jack is back out in the mountains and we're still climbing together." (*Sources: David Steele and Jack Beard.*)

NEVADA

FALL ON ROCK | Inadequate Protection
Red Rock Canyon National Conservation Area, Dark Shadows

On May 6, two teams (Mike and Keith, Chris and Jeff, all experienced climbers) did the full Dark Shadows (5.8, 10 pitches). Mike and Keith topped out about 5 p.m., with the second party trailing 15 to 30 minutes behind. We called home to report all was well, snapped some pics, and scouted the route down. Around 5:45 p.m. we started wondering what was taking our second party so long. We yelled for them and got nothing but echo and wind noise. At 6 p.m. we rigged a rope off a big pine tree to lower down the route and see about Chris and Jeff. As we extended over the edge, we heard calls for help. We scrambled back up, cleaned our gear, and rapped off the tree.

With a 70-meter rope, we were unable to reach Jeff, who had fallen in the middle of the ninth pitch while leading. We built an interim anchor and Mike rapped down to Jeff. He was conscious, standing on a slopping ledge, and had secured himself and rigged a sling for his right arm. He knew his elbow and some ribs were broken. We later learned he had been unconscious and had a broken scapula and cracked vertebrae. (All the climbers were wearing helmets.) He was in a lot of pain and moaned every time he took a deep breath, which we attributed to the broken ribs.

Before falling, Jeff reported, he had decided he did not like a certain nut placement and had moved up a bit to find better pro. When he fell, the nut popped and he went 20 feet to the ledge.

Communication was a problem, with Keith above Mike and Jeff, and Chris below. With much difficulty, Mike was able to ask Chris to untie from his end of their 70-meter half ropes. With even more difficulty communicating, we sent the ropes up for Keith to rig a rappel. This would get us all to Chris' belay stance in one rappel. We lowered Jeff to Chris and then joined them.

Led by Jeff's feeling that he could endure the pain, we decided to continue to self-rescue, leaving various pieces of gear until we got to the bolted anchors on the lower pitches. Jeff preferred controlling his own descent on rappel. He was in a lot of pain, but otherwise able to evaluate and communicate as we rigged his raps. We sent one party down for a fireman's belay and then Jeff would cast off second. (Editor's note: In the "fireman's belay," a climber below the rappel can control the speed of the rappeller's descent by adding tension to the ropes, making them more resistant to passing through the rappel device.)

Darkness arrived at the top of pitch five, and although we all had headlamps it became harder to find the fixed anchors. We were able to rap to the top of pitch two before the 70-meter half ropes got stuck in the fixed anchors on top of station four. We decided to continue with our remaining 70-meter rope, finally reaching the ground at 1 a.m. We hiked approximately three miles to the car and drove to the hospital in Las Vegas. To our surprise, Jeff was released later the same day.

ANALYSIS

We needed a better communication plan. In Red Rock climbers are often out of sight of the belayer, and voice communication is often difficult to impossible. We had worked out a series of rope tugs to communicate, but backup radios would have been wise.

Our decision to self-rescue, based on how we assessed Jeff's condition, was the right one. Some members of our team had wilderness medical training, and we all had self-rescue skills, although some not recently practiced. We made several decisions earlier in the day that played out favorably. We planned to stay in reasonable proximity of each other, let others pass if needed (one group did), and when one team reached the top we would wait for the second team. These decisions enabled us to get off the mountain relatively efficiently. (*Source: Mike Harris.*)

RAPPEL ERROR | Inadequate Anchor
Red Rock National Conservation Area, Oak Creek Canyon

On December 26, three climbers finished the classic three-pitch route Johnny Vegas (5.7) in Red Rock's Oak Creek Canyon. The three stopped for a brief lunch at about 11 a.m. on the terrace at the top of Johnny Vegas to consider whether they should continue up Solar Slab or rappel to the ground. Because of the cold and windy conditions, they decided to rappel the Solar Slab Gully instead of climbing any higher. The two females in the party made the first rappel from a less-commonly used bolted anchor to safely reach an anchor on a large, bushy ledge. As the third member rappelled to join them, he fell approximately 100 feet, landing on the ledge where they were waiting. His partners called for help with a cell phone. Despite efforts to revive their fallen partner, he was deceased when LVMPD Search and Rescue (SAR) personnel arrived. The two uninjured climbers were assisted down the two remaining rappels by SAR.

ANALYSIS

It is difficult to definitively determine the cause of the victim's fall. There was no evidence of a failure in the anchor or a piece of personal equipment. The distance from the rappel anchor to the ledge below is greater than 100 feet, and their dynamic lead rope was measured to be 200 feet in length. The victim was carrying a 6mm "pull cord," sometimes used by climbers to retrieve a lead rope from below. Strangely, the pull cord and the primary rope were not connected.

It is believed the victim initially tied the lead rope to the anchor and his partners individually rappelled on this single strand to the ledge. He then likely rearranged the rappel setup to include the pull cord, so that he could retrieve the main rope after completing the rappel. Because the two-bolt anchor and chains remained intact but the ropes were not connected, it seems that when he weighted the lead rope it was not supported by the anchor and allowed him to fall to the ledge below.

Upon inspection, the lead rope and pull cord had no damage. The lead rope had no knots or hitches. The pull cord had a figure 8 on a bight at one end that was clipped into a closed and locked screw-gate carabiner. The climber's partners report that when he struck the ledge the lead rope was threaded through his rappel device, approximately 15 feet from the end that had been secured to the anchor, but they disconnected him to facilitate CPR.

The evidence suggests he attempted to set up a "biner block" rappel anchor, threading the lead rope through the anchor bolts and then tying it to the carabiner clipped to the pull cord. He likely either failed to connect the two ropes, tied the lead rope to the carabiner improperly, or tied the wrong knot (e.g., a Munter hitch instead of a clove hitch. See page 39 for a report of a similar rappelling accident and an illustration of a "biner block" rappel anchor.) (*Source: Las Vegas Metropolitan Police Department Search and Rescue.*)

Editor's note: Another Red Rock rappelling fatality occurred in March, when Todd Jenkins, 41, fell to the ground in Black Velvet Canyon. The experienced climber had completed a sport route that was too long for lowering. He went off-belay and threaded the rope at the anchor, intending to rappel once to a midway anchor and then make a second rappel to the ground. However, the rope strands for his first rappel apparently were uneven in length.

As he was cleaning quickdraws en route to the midway anchor, he did not notice the shorter rope end pass through his rappel device, causing him to fall to the ground. Greater care with ensuring the rope lengths were even or tying stopper knots in the ends likely could have prevented this tragic accident.

NEW HAMPSHIRE

EXPOSURE | Inadequate Equipment
Presidential Range, Mt. Adams

At 5 a.m. on February 15, Kate Matrosova, 32, of New York City, was dropped off at the Appalachia parking lot by her husband. She planned a one-day winter traverse of the northern Presidential Range, a technically moderate mountaineering objective that often has severe weather. The Mount Washington Observatory, ten miles south of Matrosova's starting point, called for gusts up to 125 mph and wind-chill values of -70°F. Matrosova made her way up the Valley Way trail and began an ascent of Mt. Adams, a smaller but exposed peak.

It appears Matrosova was beaten back from the 5,774-foot summit by the extremely high winds. She made her way back down the eastern side of Adams, where she reached the col between Adams and Mt. Madison, a half-mile above treeline. There is an Appalachian Mountain Club hut in this col, but it is closed for winter and offers no shelter. At around 3:30 p.m., Matrosova turned on her SPOT emergency locater beacon, initiating a search effort. Several New Hampshire Fish and Game officers and a small team from the Mountain Rescue Service headed up the trail at around 7 p.m. The team began their search just below treeline, where a second beacon signal had suggested Matrosova might have sought shelter. After several hours of searching, it became clear the beacon was sending faulty messages. The rescue team turned back in worsening weather.

A larger rescue team, including members of Androscoggin Valley Search and Rescue, hiked up the next day in equally bad conditions. The wind gusted around 100 mph. At around 2 p.m. Matrosova's body was found at Star Lake—painfully

Mt. Adams from Mt. Madison. Ice-covered Star Lake, where Kate Matrosova was found, is at the foot of Adams' summit cone, left of the closed AMC hut. *Northeast Hikes*

close to Matrosova's original SPOT beacon position. She appeared to have been blown over by a strong gust of wind and was found with her headlamp on. The likely cause of death was hypothermia. (*Sources: SAR personnel and news reports.*)

ANALYSIS

Severe wind and freezing temperatures were the main contributing factors in Matrosova's death. Matrosova was an experienced mountaineer, having climbed

Rainer, Denali, and Aconcagua, but her lightweight, in-a-day approach to the traverse left her without the equipment to bivouac in such conditions. Knowing the weather forecast, recognizing when the weather is too extreme to continue, and altering a plan accordingly are extremely important parts of any mountaineering endeavor. The Mount Washington Observatory's website (*www.mwobs.org*) posts an accurate forecast each morning on temperature, wind speed, and wind chill for these mountains.

Carrying an emergency locater beacon on a solo hike or climb can increase safety, but not as much as a partner or bivouac gear. Moreover, this incident shows that beacon signals can be misleading to searchers, and they cannot be relied upon as your first line of defense. (*Source: The Editors.*)

FALL ON ROCK | Inadequate Experience
Echo Lake State Park, Whitehorse Ledge

Two climbers chose Whitehorse's classic Standard Route (5.5) as an introduction to multi-pitch climbing. They set off the morning of August 29 equipped with a traditional rack and a single rope. At around 3 or 4 in the afternoon, the lead climber aided through the crux sixth pitch, leaving an aider attached to a fixed piton to ease the passage for the second. The second climber fell out of the aid sling and slammed into the wall. While she sustained no significant injuries, she was rattled. Upon reaching the belay, the climber refused to continue. Unable to rappel with their single line, the pair waited on the massive tree ledge below the seventh pitch of the route. Three hundred feet of 5.1 to 5.2 terrain led to the summit of Whitehorse Ledge from this location.

At around 8 p.m., three members of the Mountain Rescue Service ascended Standard Route and made several tandem rappels with the two climbers to the base of Whitehorse Ledge. Of note was the fact that one climber's harness was not doubled back when we reached him.

ANALYSIS
Inexperience and poor planning skills necessitated this rescue. It is essential that climbers have goals and terrain that mirror their experience. Neither climber had made a rappel prior to this outing (the tandem rappels were their first). Seeking proper instruction or choosing less committing goals when learning is a good way to avoid rescues. (*Source: The Editors.*)

FALL ON ROCK | Inadequate Protection
Barber Wall, Cathedral Ledge State Park

On Sunday, August 30, a climber fell 40 feet near the top of Double Vee, a popular but tricky-to-protect 5.9 at the Barber Wall on Cathedral Ledge. While he had four pieces of protection in, all but one (a number three Camalot ten feet above the ground) ripped out, resulting in a ground fall. An EMT was at the Barber Wall, and within minutes several members of the Mountain Rescue Service and volunteers had arrived on scene as well. After fixing ropes across a few exposed spots, backboarding the patient and placing him in a litter, MRS members and volunteers raised the litter to the top of Cathedral Ledge to a waiting ambulance.

ANALYSIS

This route has had a few accidents in recent years. The top is very difficult to protect and insecure for the grade. Given this, the leader must be extremely comfortable on the terrain. The climber might have been able to retreat and reconsider his options before committing to the tricky terrain and bad protection above. Taking the time to place a few good pieces in the middle of the route may also have prevented a ground fall. Not moving above gear that's suspect is a good way to prevent a fall like this from happening. (*Source: The Editors.*)

Editor's note: A similar accident occurred at the North End of Cathedral Ledge in June, when a 25-year-old man leading Kiddy Crack (5.7) pulled two pieces of protection and fell a reported 50 feet to the ground. He was wearing a helmet, which may have prevented a serious head injury.

NEW YORK

FALL ON ROCK | Inadequate Protection, Inexperience
Adirondacks, Wallface

On August 17, a 23-year-old male climber fell while leading the second pitch of Diagonal (5.8, seven pitches) on Wallface, a 700-foot cliff five miles from the trailhead. The leader had gotten off-route on the broken and bushy second pitch (5.5, with harder variations). Reportedly, he was hanging on a cam and yelling up to other climbers for directions when the cam pulled out. He may have pulled one or more additional protection pieces. He fell an estimated 60 to 80 feet, likely hitting some ledges and "crashing through a small tree island," which may have slowed the fall and prevented a fatal accident. He was wearing a helmet. The fall stopped 200 feet above the ground, about 40 feet above the top of the first pitch.

Two climbers on the third pitch rappelled to help the patient and his partner. There was no cell phone signal on the cliff, but, fortuitously, a friend of the climbers, watching them from a point near Indian Pass, saw the fall and called for help. A

The Diagonal follows a long ramp line in the left center of Wallface. The 2015 accident occurred on the tree-dotted pitches below the ramp. *Jim Lawyer* ranger and volunteer climber rescuer were inserted by helicopter near the foot of the cliff and climbed the first pitch to reach the scene, reaching the ledge at 5:20 p.m. A litter was raised to the ledge, and a system was rigged to lower the climber in the litter to the scree slope below.

Additional rangers had arrived on scene, and they helped carry the litter with the injured climber down the scree to an area where a helicopter could hoist the litter aboard and transport the climber to the hospital. (*Sources: Climbers and rescuers at the scene, N.Y. Department of Environmental Conservation report, news reports.*)

ANALYSIS

According to one of the other climbers on the route that day, this was not only the rescued party's first multi-pitch climb but also its first trad climbing experience. It would have been better to develop these on shorter routes much closer to the road than a large backcountry cliff like Wallface, where loose or wet rock, route-finding challenges, time pressure, and weather concerns add several layers of difficulty and seriousness to a climb. (*Source: The Editors.*)

FALL ON ROCK | Insect Stings
Shawangunks, Near Trapps

Jason, an experienced local guide, and his technically competent client decided to climb in the Near Trapps on August 7. After two multi-pitch warmup climbs, the next objective was the two-pitch Layback. At the top of the first pitch (5.5), Jason built a three-piece anchor at a good-size ledge and brought up his client. From there, the route climbs up easy, blocky terrain before traversing right at 5.4.

After climbing up ten feet, Jason stepped on a rocking block and his client began to notice swarming wasps (or similar stinging insects.) As soon as he began to feel stings, Jason attempted to climb back to the belay. He reached for the anchor but grabbed something unsupportive and fell, landing hard on his feet on the belay ledge. Jason immediately saw that his right distal tibia was exposed through his skin above the sock, and that his right foot was very externally rotated.

Jason yelled to friends at the base to contact 911, request paramedics, and then call the Mohonk Preserve rangers. He immediately initiated a self-rescue. Utilizing the anchor he had built, he rigged his own rappel and backup, and pre-rigged his client's rappel above that. Jason was able to safely rappel with the assistance of a fireman's belay and helpful hands on the ground. His client arrived on the ground, similarly backed up during her rappel, without incident. Mohonk Preserve rangers completed a carry-out to a waiting ambulance.

ANALYSIS

Climbers face many environmental objective hazards, including wildlife. The best way to mitigate such risks is through awareness—there are few practical methods of physical protection. In some cases the community may become aware of wildlife presence, and that information may be accessible online or elsewhere to those who seek it out. This incident was at the start of what became a particularly aggressive wasp and bee season in the Gunks, with at least one very popular climb closed due to their presence. Climbers with known severe allergies should carry an EpiPen or similar emergency treatment to the crag or even on routes. (*Source: The Editors.*)

BASIC INJURY ASSESSMENT
HOW TO HELP BEFORE HELP ARRIVES

By R. Bryan Simon

While most climbers are not medical professionals, climbers are well disposed to dealing with situations that require focus and psychological strength. Transitioning these skills to an emergency situation can speed treatment and evacuation of an injured partner.

A climber with little or no medical training can use several methods to assess someone who is injured, including the one described below. Whatever method you learn, it's most important to know it by heart and use it in an emergency. It will save time, focus your efforts, and help first responders understand the situation. Staying calm and following these steps might be the difference between life and death.

PROTECT YOURSELF
Before you can begin to assess and treat an injured climber, you must first ensure that you and your partners are safe. This includes building a solid anchor and protecting yourself against rockfall, avalanche danger, and other environmental hazards.

CALL FOR HELP
If it is obvious that help will be needed (e.g., any serious or life-threatening injury), do not hesitate to call 911 immediately. Try to have the following information ready for the operator:
- Casualties (number of injured, types of injuries)
- Hazards (rockfall, avalanche, strong winds)
- Access and location (coordinates, nearest trailhead, route name)

ASSESS THE PATIENT
Now take a closer look for life-threatening injuries, following the MARCH mnemonic. If possible, write down the details to aid medical responders.

(M) Massive Hemorrhage
Is there massive bleeding? A thorough assessment for internal and external bleeding should be conducted, starting at the head and working downward to the feet. Blood is a finite resource and cannot be replaced in the backcountry; therefore, stopping massive bleeding is essential. Minor bleeding or oozing from superficial wounds is of little concern and can be treated after a full initial assessment for life-threatening injuries is completed.

Internal areas where bleeding can occur include the chest, abdomen, retroperitoneal space (flanks), pelvis, and thighs. Identification of internal bleeding is difficult for the layperson, but wounds and significant bruising in these areas are indicators. Deformity and swelling of the thigh indicate a femur fracture and associated blood loss. Other indicators of internal blood loss include low blood pressure, thready or absent pulse, pale skin, and reduced level of consciousness over time.

External bleeding is easier to identify, but be sure to check inside layers of clothing. (Today's technical gear is meant to keep water out, but it also has the ability to trap bleeding against the skin.) If severe external bleeding is detected, apply direct pressure using the cleanest material available and elevate the wound if possible. An improvised tourniquet may be needed to stop bleeding.

(A) Airway with C-Spine / Assess Consciousness

Is air moving in and out of the injured climber's mouth or nose? Look at the chest and listen and feel for air movement. If not, you may need to open the airway using a jaw thrust (lifting the chin forward), find and remove any obstructions in the mouth, and stabilize the cervical spine (C-spine). If there is still no air movement, begin CPR. Stabilization of the C-spine is necessary in any instance where the head, neck, or spine may have sustained damage.

This is also a good time to assess consciousness. Using the mnemonic AVPU is a quick and easy way to check for head injuries. (For additional detail, see "Essentials: Head Injuries" in Accidents 2015.)

- **A** Awake (alert and oriented to person, place, time, and event)
- **V** Responds to Verbal stimuli (awakens, withdraws, or moans when spoken to)
- **P** Responds to Painful stimuli (awakens, withdraws, or moans in response to pain)
- **U** Unresponsive (no response to any stimuli)

(R) Respiration

Is the patient breathing? Check for chest rise. If the patient has labored breathing or is breathing rapidly, position him or her with the head/chest up, in a position of comfort. Reassure the patient and give oxygen (if available). If he or she is not breathing, begin rescue breaths.

(C) Circulation

Does the patient have a pulse? The best areas to feel a pulse are the arteries in the neck (carotid), the wrist (radial), or the groin (femoral). If the patient does not have a pulse, begin CPR.

(H) Hypothermia/Hyperthermia and Hike vs. Helicopter

Once immediate life-threatening emergencies are addressed, the patient should be protected from the elements to prevent hypothermia or hyperthermia. Patients are often immobile and may have significant portions of their body exposed to the elements during care, causing them to become too cold or hot.

The final decision is whether the injuries require helicopter evacuation or if the patient can hike or be carried to a trailhead. This decision is often made in conjunction with rescue personnel by phone. Once they are at the scene, they will likely make the decision based upon their knowledge of resources and terrain.

Many books and courses teach wilderness first aid and wilderness medicine skills, and can help prepare you for accidents at the crag or on a mountain. At a minimum, take a CPR course—they are cheap, widely available, and can save a life.

R. Bryan Simon, a registered nurse and co-owner of Vertical Medicine Resources, is co-author of the upcoming book Vertical Aid: Essential Wilderness Medicine for Climbers, Trekkers, and Alpinists.

FALL ON ROCK | Inadequate Protection
Shawangunks, The Trapps

On Labor Day I planned to lead Thin Slabs for the first time, having only followed the climb once before. We wanted to do the direct start (5.7) and the challenging direct finish (5.7+). I made it through the first hard moves on pitch one clean, with good gear. My buddy led pitch two to the Grand Traverse Ledge. We looked at the direct finish for a while and decided to go for it. I got a good piece in and clipped the first two pins along the rightward traverse under the roof with long runners, then backed down to the corner to rest. I did not clip the last pin since I'd heard it was sketchy and saw it was probably the weakest one.

Once I was ready, I went for it and made the moves all the way out to the end. Just as I brought my right foot up to finish the crux it slipped, my hand came off, and I was swinging in space. We estimated it was about a 12-foot pendulum fall. My right foot hit first—I heard a pop and saw my ankle dislocate. Fortunately, my partner, Skip Thompson, kept a cool head. He lowered me to the ledge, found a long stick as a crutch, and set me up for a lower on our 70-meter rope. As I was lowered, I used the stick to keep my foot off the wall and stay in balance. Once on the ground we called 911. At the hospital, X-rays showed a fracture and dislocation, which the ER doctor reduced. The next day I had surgery to put in three screws.

ANALYSIS
This climb is rated 5.7+, and I have led 5.8 at the Gunks, so it was within my ability. Also, I had followed this climb without falling. Placing one more cam would have limited my swing and probably have prevented an injury. Clipping the last pin might have helped. The good news is that all the gear I clipped held. (*Source: Paul Alberti.*)

ANNUAL SUMMARY
Shawangunks (Mohonk Preserve)

At the Mohonk Preserve there were 27 climbing-related incidents in 2015, including both bouldering and soloing. Two required high-angle rescues, and 12 required steep-angle extrications. In many cases, common safety measures might have lessened the severity or prevented the incident altogether.

There were seven reported bouldering injuries, all in the Trapps area. Injuries were caused from falls as low as four feet (Boxcar Traverse) and as high as 13 feet (Boulder of the Gods). Witness reports commonly stated there were either no spotters present or spotters were using incorrect technique at the time the injuries occurred. These included lower leg fractures and spinal and head injuries.

A 27-year-old climber sustained fractures to the lumbar spine while rappelling off Horseman, a 5.5 in the Trapps. The climber fell approximately 15 feet. It is thought the rappel was done with uneven rope ends.

Several accidents occurred when soloing climbers fell or hikers scrambled into terrain harder than fourth class and fell. A soloing fatality occurred when an experienced 46-year-old climber fell 50 feet or more feet while soloing Cascading Crystal Kaleidoscope (5.7) in the Trapps. The climber was wearing a harness with a dynamic rope tied to a loop on its back. The cause of the fall is unknown, but it is thought the climber had reached the Grand Traverse Ledge when he fell.

A serious injury took place when a 28-year-old climber fell leading the start of CCK Direct, which starts off the GT ledge. The climber fell approximately 10 feet and sustained an open lower leg fracture. In several other accidents, lower leg fractures were sustained when climbers impacted a ledge, despite being belayed.

Probably 999 times out of 1,000 you won't need stopper knots, a good spot, extra gear right off the deck, and the many other steps we take to keep us safer while climbing. Not every situation demands every measure—situational awareness in a vertical environment of any height is key. But every time a safety measure is not considered, there in an increase in the likelihood of an accident. Unlike us, gravity never takes a rest day. (*Source: Andrew Bajardi, Chief Ranger, Mohonk Preserve.*)

NORTH CAROLINA

STRANDED | Darkness, Inadequate Communication
Hanging Rock State Park, Moore's Wall

After completing one climb on September 17, Eli Huneycutt (20) and Will Apple (36) began climbing Zoo View (5.7+), a classic two-pitch route. Huneycutt successfully led the first pitch to the Crow's Nest belay ledge. Apple began the second pitch, but was unable to negotiate a roof section. It was becoming dark and the pair decided to retreat. Apple left some gear under the roof so he could retreat to the Crow's Nest. From here they were able to rappel to the ground.

Before leaving the area, they decided to retrieve the gear they'd left behind. They scrambled to the top of the route and set up a rappel with their 70-meter rope. Apple descended over the roof and then realized the doubled rope (with rope ends knotted) was too short to reach the Crow's Nest. Huneycutt noted, "All of a sudden he says, 'I'm at the end of my rope, literally'.... I really got scared at one point where he was able to touch the rock wall and was able to stand up. I felt the weight go off of the rope and yelled down to him, 'Are you still there?'"

The confused communication caused Huneycutt to call rescuers and say he and his climbing partner were stranded on Moore's Wall, when in fact Apple had already begun a self-rescue. Apple executed a leg wrap with the remaining rope to halt his rappel and was able to retrieve the gear left behind. Using the equipment he had with him (mostly slings and carabiners), he was able to ascend the rope more than 100 feet, taking approximately one hour to rejoin Huneycutt. They met rescuers as they were walking out the trail. (*Sources: Will Apple, news reports.*)

ANALYSIS

Climbers should familiarize themselves with descent routes and equipment requirements before attempting an unknown descent. A second rope would have been helpful in this situation, along with a headlamp. (Apple was able to use his smartphone as a light source.) In most cases, attempts at self-rescue should be exhausted before calling for rescue. With some effort and improvisation, Apple successfully got himself out of a difficult spot. Once they were both on top, the climbers should have called back to inform rescuers they were safe. (*Sources: Will Apple, Karsten Delap, Aram Attarian.*)

FALL ON ROCK | Anchor Knot Failure
Pisgah National Forest, Looking Glass Rock

On July 7, Transylvania County Rescue Team received a call at 3:36 p.m. regarding a fall with injury at the South Side of Looking Glass Rock. Wilderness First Responders were on scene when I (Karsten Delap) arrived at 4:08 p.m. to find the patient (male, early 20s) supine, with his girlfriend holding C-spine. The patient was not wearing a helmet, but said he did not hit his head and had not lost consciousness. He had an open fracture (already bandaged) to the right tibula/fibula and possible fracture to the left tib/fib as well as the left ankle.

Once other rescuers arrived, we transported the patient to the trailhead via wheeled Stokes basket. Fox Mountain Guides provided steep-angle belays on the trail when necessary. Care was turned over to flight medics, and the patient proceeded to the landing zone in an ambulance.

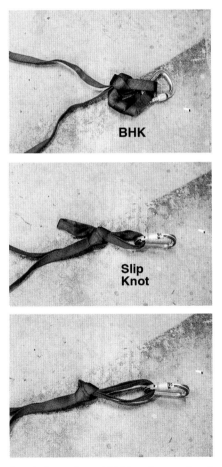

(Top) Correctly tied BHK, with extra "ear" of webbing (lower loop in photo) clipped to the master point for safekeeping. **(Middle)** Incorrectly tied master-point knot, creating a slipknot with no backup. **(Bottom)** Under load, the extra ear of the slipknot pulls through and the knot fails. *Karsten Delap*

ANALYSIS

The climbers had planned to set up a top-rope from Stage Ledge on Looking Glass' South Side. They scrambled to the ledge, built an anchor using two cams, and one of the climbers proceeded to lean back on the rappel. At this point, the climber stated, he felt the knot at the master point slip, hold for a second, and then he started to fall.

I took photos of the scene at the base of the route and on top. When the climber hit the ground, his rappel rope was still threaded through the device clipped to his harness. Two locking carabiners, still locked, were clipped to the rope. On top, two nylon slings that were tied together to extend toward the lip remained connected to the anchor. At the other end was an overhand knot forming a loop.

The evidence shows that the climber attempted to tie a BHK (Big Honking Knot) for a master point. Tied correctly, this overhand knot creates two bights of webbing or rope to provide redundant material at the master point. However, it is possible to tie the knot incorrectly and create a slipknot that looks similar but will fail under load. Check your knots before trusting them! (*Source: Karsten Delap, Fox Mountain Guides.*)

OREGON

FALL ON SNOW | Inadequate Equipment
Mt. Hood, South Side

On January 7, while descending the South Side Route, at about 9,700 feet, Edward Trompke, 62, fell and slid about 200 feet, injuring his shoulder. His son, climbing with him, alerted authorities with a 911 call, saying the fall was caused by a loose crampon.

Teams from Portland Mountain Rescue and American Medical Response lowered the subject in a litter to the ski area, where Timberline professional patrollers transported the climber to an awaiting ambulance.

ANALYSIS

For crampons to be safe and effective, they must be properly sized and firmly fastened to the climbing boot, and straps and clothing must be tightened or secured so they can't cause the climber to trip and fall. After crampons are donned, kicking them against hard snow and rapping the sides with an ice axe can help determine if they are securely attached. (*Source: Jeff Scheetz, Portland Mountain Rescue.*)

The Mazama Chute area near the top of Mt. Hood's South Side Route, with a rescue team attending to climbers who have fallen. Some of the rescuers have formed a "human wall" to guard the responders and patients against small falling rocks and ice. *Portland Mountain Rescue*

FALL ON SNOW | Failure to Self-Arrest
Mt. Hood, South Side

While descending the Mazama Chute on January 31, a roped team of two (ages 39 and 43) fell and suffered ankle and lower leg fractures. It is believed the upper climber lost her footing during a rest break and slid toward the lower climber. Rather than firmly anchoring himself to brace for the fall, the lower climber attempted to grab the falling partner. Neither climber was able to arrest, and the slide ended about 500 feet lower in the Hot Rocks area.

The accident was witnessed by Portland Mountain Rescue personnel training nearby. The subjects were treated and evacuated to a lower part of the glacier, where they were picked up by an Army National Guard helicopter.

ANALYSIS

On the 50° snow slope where the slide initiated, climbers must be proficient at ice axe self-arrest and roped team arrest. An unarrested fall of 10 to 20 feet develops too much energy to be stopped by tackling. The lower climber would have had more success if he had immediately fallen into the self-arrest position and let the rope catch the falling partner. This climb and descent are normally done without belays or protection. An unarrested roped fall may

Rescuers work to extract a climber who slid 450 feet and dropped into a fumarole after a crampon malfunction. *Erik Broms / Portland Mountain Rescue*

pull off multiple climbers and/or entangle other teams on this busy climb. (*Source: Jeff Scheetz, Portland Mountain Rescue.*)

Editor's note: On the same day, also in the Mazama Chute, a 29-year-old solo climber fell approximately 450 feet, ending his slide in a fumarole, when a crampon malfunction prompted him to stop his descent and then slip. He was unable to self-arrest. Portland Mountain Rescue personnel observed the fall and pulled him from the fumarole 26 minutes later. The climber had only minor injuries and was lucky the fumarole gases were non-lethal.

ROCKFALL
Mt. Hood, South Side

Casey Ferguson, age 27, was struck by a boulder while descending a chute just below the summit on June 14. The microwave-size rock fractured her lower leg. Three other companions managed to dodge the boulder, after a climber above them yelled, "Rock!" Ferguson's teammates and nearby climbers applied a splint and raised her about 150 feet back to the summit, the nearest level ground. After a 911 call, American Medical Response (AMR) paramedics hiked to the summit to provide professional treatment and request an air evacuation. A Portland Mountain Rescue (PMR) team also arrived to support a ground evacuation if necessary. Eventually, a Blackhawk helicopter performed a litter hoist from an altitude of 11,300 feet and flew the patient to a Portland hospital.

ANALYSIS

The rockfall occurred at 9:30 a.m. in a south-facing chute. Although this was before the peak heating caused by the summer sun, there was still enough warming to loosen the boulder. Prudent climbers often start their climb about 2 a.m., allowing for a safe descent before warming of the upper rim and subsequent rockfall hazard. Such a start also gets them off the upper route before the majority of climbers queue for the summit. The climber who shouted "Rock!" may have helped prevent other injuries. (*Jeff Scheetz, Portland Mountain Rescue.*)

Editor's note: On June 4, a 66-year-old, experienced climber slipped at around 10,500 feet on the South Side Route, and the unroped climber fell about 400 feet to the Hot Rocks area. His party quickly reached him and attempted CPR, but were unable to revive him. The climber did not attempt self-arrest, suggesting the possibility that a medical incident triggered the fall.

FALL ON ICE
Mt. Jefferson, Jefferson Park Glacier

A husband and wife team of experienced climbers, ages 32 and 29, were attempting to summit via the Jefferson Park Glacier on November 29. The two had to maneuver around a crevasse field and past an area of rockfall, and they encountered much hard ice on the glacier surface. They crossed over to the Whitewater Glacier in hopes of finding sun and better snow conditions, but at 1:45 p.m., around 9,600 feet, they decided to turn back. After some discussion they elected to downclimb the way they had come.

By this point the climbers were getting tired, and the man began cutting steps into the ice to help his wife move down steep sections more easily. He would kick his crampons into the ice to get solid footing, then cut a step with his ice axe, move down a few feet, and do it again. At 3 p.m., while cutting one of these steps, the climber slipped and was unable to self-arrest. He fell approximately 500 feet and slid into a crevasse, at about 8,800 feet, suffering fatal injuries. The woman called for help via text message and spent the night on the mountain in difficult conditions before a team from Corvallis Mountain Rescue Unit could reach her early on Monday. The victim's remains were recovered by helicopter the following day. (*Sources: Corvallis Mountain Rescue Unit and news reports.*)

ANALYSIS
Climbers have to be ready to adapt to changing or unexpected conditions, either by roping up (and belaying if necessary) or by retreating before climbing into difficulty. These two climbers were traveling unroped, and rescuers agreed this was not inappropriate for the route they were climbing: "We felt that this team of climbers were doing things right but fell victim to a tragic accident." (*Source: The Editors.*)

Editor's note: Another fatality on a central Oregon volcano occurred on September 20. A 22-year-old man fell approximately 700 feet after unroping atop the small summit pinnacle of Three Fingered Jack. Appropriate anchor systems should be maintained in such exposed locations.

ROCKFALL
Mt. Washington

In the evening of October 11, a 20-year-old solo climber was hit in the head by rockfall while rappelling the summit block of this 7,795-foot volcano. This caused her to fall about 15 feet and badly injure a knee. The climber was able to descend to about 6,200 feet, but could not continue. She called for help at around 11:25 p.m., and her cell phone battery then died. Rescuers were able to locate her around 7 a.m. Because of the nature of her injuries and the rugged location, she was airlifted from the scene by Oregon Army National Guard helicopter. (*Source: Corvallis Mountain Rescue Unit and news reports.*)

The rocky summit of 7,795-foot Mt. Washington in central Oregon. There were three separate rockfall injuries to climbers on this peak in 2015. *Todd Shechter / Corvallis Mountain Rescue Unit*

ANALYSIS

A similar accident occurred on Mt. Washington in July, when a climber was hit by rockfall while rappelling the upper mountain. Both incidents suggest the importance of using a backup, such as a friction hitch, when rappelling in areas of loose rock. The friction hitch can prevent a climber from falling to the end of the ropes if incapacitated.

In August, another climber was hit by rockfall while hiking the descent trail from Mt. Washington. On mountains with known rockfall dangers, helmets are mandatory and climbing or descending underneath other parties is unwise. (*Source: The Editors.*)

ROCKFALL | Inexperience
Smith Rock State Park, Picnic Lunch Wall

On March 14, a large group of climbers from the Yale University Climbing Club was climbing at Smith Rock. Two climbers headed up Voyage of the Cow Dog, a three-pitch 5.9. One of them (age 20) was following the third pitch when he dislodged a microwave-size block above shoulder level. The rock fell and lacerated his right lower leg to the point where a bone was visible. He was unable to rappel without assistance, so the climbers called 911 for help. Rescue teams responded and assisted with the rappel.

ANALYSIS

Voyage of the Cow Dog does not see the same level of traffic as many of Smith Rock's routes, and the Picnic Lunch Wall is known for having some poorer rock. This climber had little outdoor experience and thus likely had limited experience with loose holds. Test holds by rapping on them with the palm or knuckles, listening for hollow sounds and watching for movement. With suspect blocks, always pull down and not out. (*Source: Matt Crawford, Deschutes County Sheriff's Office Search and Rescue.*)

FALL ON ROCK | Inadequate Protection
Smith Rock State Park, Christian Brothers

Keith Kowalczykowski, 30, was leading Hesitation Blues, a 5.10b face and finger crack, on April 18. He clipped the route's two bolts, at approximately 15 and 25 feet, then placed a small cam at 30 to 35 feet. He placed a fourth piece (type unknown) and then fell, pulling the fourth piece from the wall. The rope either was not clipped to the cam below or became detached, and the top bolt was too low on the route to keep Kowalczykowski from hitting the ground, after falling at least 40 feet. He suffered a skull fracture and concussion.

A climber appears to have accidentally clipped his extension sling back into the small cam he placed to protect a 5.10 climb at Smith Rock, instead of clipping the sling to the lead rope. *Matt Crawford*

ANALYSIS

Kowalczykowski was unable to describe the placement of the third piece after the incident, but it remained on the route and was examined afterward. The piece had been extended with a shoulder-length sling attached to the cam with a carabiner. A second carabiner, intended to clip the rope, was attached to the cam's sling adjacent to the first biner, suggesting the climber accidentally clipped the sling of the cam instead of the rope. Whether this mistake was made in haste or because the climber was pumped, he might have caught the error if he had glanced at the placement before continuing up the route. Placing additional pro, at shorter intervals, could have prevented a long fall when the top piece failed. (*Source: Matt Crawford, Deschutes County Sheriff's Office Search and Rescue.*)

ANIMAL BITE
Smith Rock State Park, Lower Gorge

On June 23, Bryan Simon (39) was bitten by a bat (species unknown) while climbing Pet Cemetery, a 5.11b sport route at the Catwalk Cliff of the Lower Gorge. After clipping the fifth bolt, the climber placed a hand under a flake on the left side of the route. Multiple bats flew from the flake, and Simon pulled his hand back to reveal three bleeding wounds, on the middle, ring, and pinkie fingers of his left hand. After asking his belayer to "take," he lowered to the ground, where they immediately began to irrigate the wounds with clean water. Knowing that bats are carriers of the rabies virus, they hiked out of the gorge and called area hospitals to ascertain which had post-exposure prophylaxis (PEP) for rabies available. The climber received the full series of PEP over the next four weeks.

ANALYSIS
Though fairly uncommon, these encounters should be taken seriously. Rabies is a fatal viral disease that must be treated promptly if suspected. Bats are a common reservoir of the rabies virus, and their habitat includes the flakes, cracks, and crevices in climbing areas. If you suspect a bite or scratch by a bat or other mammal that could carry the virus, clean the wound thoroughly with copious amounts of water and/or providone-iodine. Seek medical evaluation as soon as possible, and begin post-exposure prophylaxis if indicated. (*Source: R. Bryan Simon.*)

FALL ON ROCK | Inadequate Protection
Smith Rock State Park, Christian Brothers

On September 3, Peter Kettering, 61, was starting up what he believed was Revelations (5.9). In fact, he was mistakenly leading the harder climb Irreverence (5.10a). Just before clipping the first bolt, Kettering fell 12 to 15 feet to the ground. Kettering injured both ankles in the fall and was carried to an ambulance.

ANALYSIS
Smith Rock is known for high first bolts. The use of a spotter or bouldering pad before clipping the first bolt is recommended. Many climbers employ stick clips for routes with difficult or high first clips.

While climbing off-route or misreading the guidebook will happen, climbers should be aware of their limits and downclimb if they discover the route is more difficult than expected. (*Source: Matt Crawford, Deschutes County Sheriff's Office Search and Rescue.*)

Editor's note: A report about a fall and ankle injury at the Phoenix Buttress in June can be found at publications.americanalpineclub.org. Search "Hissing Llamas."

PENNSYLVANIA

FALL ON ROCK | Inexperience, Inadequate Belay
Birdsboro Quarry, Orange Sunshine Wall

On September 27, I took my girlfriend climbing at Birdsboro Quarry. I had been climbing for about five years, but she had never belayed a leader. I quickly showed her how to belay, then led the easiest routes, 5.3 to 5.5, and set up top-ropes so she could climb. She had not brought a helmet, so I loaned her mine. At the end of the day, I decided to sneak in something slightly harder but still well within my comfort zone: Dirty Swing, a 5.7 route on the Orange Sunshine Wall.

There were a few factors that should have deterred me from attempting this last route, including the fact that I had no chalk, I had only that day taught her how to lead belay, and she is about 80 pounds lighter than me, but I was anxious to get in as much climbing as possible.

Without anchoring her to anything, I tied in and started climbing, hardly taking a look up at the route. I made it past the crux and after the last bolt noticed an abnormally long runout before what appeared to be two sets of bolted anchors, one to my left and one to my right. I paused on a tiny ledge about 10 feet up from the last bolt, assessing the options, and the next thing I knew I was falling, probably having slipped on some loose rock. I fell about 20 feet, with my legs outstretched and knees locked, and landed straight onto my left foot on a small ledge. After flipping over, I stopped upside-down a few feet above the ground. My girlfriend had been yanked off the ground and was hanging above me. My left talus had been fractured, with my foot pointing out and to the left at a very gross angle.

First responders from Robeson Township drove me out to a waiting ambulance. I now have plates on either side of my ankle, and I wasn't able to walk for several months.

ANALYSIS

I disobeyed one of the principles of the Mountaineers' Climbing Code: "Never let judgment be overruled by desire when choosing the route or turning back." Despite not having chalk, not knowing anything about the route, and being with an inexperienced partner who weighed much less than me (and was not anchored), I went for it anyway. Midway up the climb, when I looked down and was slightly frightened to see a large loop of rope out from her belay, I simply told her to "make sure to take in some of the slack" and continued on.

Also, if I had read the comments on the Mountain Project page for this route, I would have learned of the two anchors and long runout from the last bolt, and known that the left was the one to go for. Finally, I was insanely lucky not to have hit my head. I always wear a helmet, but this day I had loaned it to my girlfriend because of the area's reputation for loose rock. (*Source: Anonymous report from the lead climber.*)

TEXAS

FALL ON ROCK | Inadequate Belay, Poor Position, No Helmet
Austin, Barton Creek Greenbelt, Gus Fruh Wall

On February 14 a climber (19) fell off the sport climb Birdland (5.10+), hitting a wide ledge about 20 feet off the ground. I was climbing nearby and saw the accident. A friend of the climber scrambled to the ledge from an adjacent climb, and then I climbed up with some extra gear. While the friend stabilized the patient's head and neck, I clove-hitched the climber's rope into the first bolt on the route. (The rope above was clipped into draws on the first and second bolts, with no quickdraw clipped to the third bolt.) The patient was conscious but confused and complaining of pain at the back of his head. I noticed a rope burn behind his left calf.

When paramedics arrived, about 15 minutes after the accident, they sent up a cervical collar, which I placed on the patient. High-angle rescuers arrived shortly afterward and set up a line to lower the patient to the ground. He was carried to the road in a litter, having suffered lacerations and a likely concussion.

ANALYSIS

Based on where the climber fell, after clipping the second bolt, it appears there may have been excessive slack in the belay rope, especially given the ledge-fall potential. The rope burn suggests the climber fell with the rope behind his leg, possibly leading to a headfirst fall. The climber told me he only had about a year of experience, primarily in gyms, and had never been to the Gus Fruh Wall. (*Source: Adam Hosterman.*)

Rockfall in Little Cottonwood Canyon smashed this belay anchor when two climbers were attached to it and a leader was above. Building a master point with independent, extension-limited arms of the sling likely saved the climbers' lives. *Carl Dec*

UTAH

ROCKFALL

Little Cottonwood Canyon, The Thumb

On February 14, Carl Dec (48), Morgan Lavery (33), and Billy Smallen (33) were enjoying unseasonably warm and sunny weather on the Standard Thumb route (III 5.7) on the Thumb formation. The three climbers were very experienced, each of them certified climbing guides. The trio had climbed the first two pitches of the route and were preparing to start the Indecent Exposure variation (5.7), a well-traveled alternative to the fourth and fifth pitches. Dec and Smallen were both attached to the anchor with the rope, clove-hitched to the master point of an 8mm Dyneema sling that was clipped to the two-bolt anchor and extension-limited with an overhand knot. As it was a spacious stance, they both were anchored with tethers between six and eight feet long.

Lavery began leading the first pitch of Indecent Exposure and was climbing through a section of double cracks when a large block dislodged. The block fell for approximately 30 feet before landing in the gully above the belay and exploding into various pieces.

Dec had scrambled up a short ways and was standing with his feet even with the anchor when the rockfall came down. He was hit in the legs and knocked down, ending up in the corner of the alcove, on his back, with a block on his chest. Smallen was able to pendulum off the anchor to the right and avoid being hit, but then swung back on the anchor after the rockfall passed.

At this point, Dec and Smallen were both hanging with their full weight on the anchor. Dec looked up to see that the rockfall had completely severed one leg of the anchor sling, and both climbers were now hanging from the master point with the intact leg of the sling clipped to the other anchor bolt. In addition to half the anchor sling being cut, the group's two ropes suffered a total of four core shots, and both belay bolts and the biners that were attached to them were smashed to varying degrees. After assessing Dec's injuries, the climbers added gear to the anchor and descended.

ANALYSIS

Anchor construction and connection is often debated, but in this scenario there is no question that clipping the master point of a redundant anchor, which would not extend, saved two lives. If a sliding X (a.k.a. magic X) had been used to equalize the sling or cordelette, without extension-limiting knots, the anchor likely would have failed completely and the climbers likely would have been killed.

Weather may have contributed to there being a loose block on this well-traveled route. The winter in Utah started off cold and wet and then went dry and warm. There was a substantial freeze/thaw cycle in the canyon that may have been enough to loosen the large block. In such areas it's good to be wary of loose rock early in the season. (*Source: Carl Dec, Red River Adventures.*)

ROCKFALL

Little Cottonwood Canyon, Pfeifferhorn

During the afternoon of February 1, Susan DeBruin (30) and Derek DeBruin (27) hiked in to Maybird Gulch above Little Cottonwood Canyon and established camp with the intention of climbing the Pfeifferhorn (a.k.a. Little Matterhorn Peak) the following day. A small amount of snow fell overnight, accompanied by winds of perhaps 40 to 50 mph. The following morning the party waited for the warmth of sunrise and then left camp around 7:30 a.m. to attempt the north ridge, approaching via the snow couloir on the east side of the ridge.

Once on the ridge, Derek established a belay in anticipation of the terrain above, largely 4th-class to low 5th-class rock, blanketed with snow and occasionally coated with verglas. The pair donned crampons and Derek began leading a series of short pitches (50–75 feet) up ledges and corners. After leading the fourth pitch, Derek established a belay and Susan began climbing.

Moments after she stepped off the ledge, she was struck by a rock on the top of her helmet. While startled and injured, she was coherent and shouted to Derek. They agreed the simplest plan would be for her to climb the 50 feet to Derek, and he could then inspect her injuries.

Susan arrived at the belay a few minutes later. Her cervical spine was free of pain, she had no sensory or neuromotor deficits, and she was completely responsive. Two of her teeth were chipped, one was cracked, and her tongue was badly bitten. She reported general pain in her teeth and jaw, and her neck muscles were stiff and painful. Her helmet suspension was completely undone, and the helmet shell had a large gouge in it.

The party rappelled from their belay stance off the east side of the ridge into a couloir. Given the low snowpack in the Wasatch that year, this couloir was barely filled, with about 10 to 15cm of faceted snow atop rock slab. Another rappel placed them in downclimbable terrain. Given the relatively slow pace of the descent, Derek became quite chilled and developed minor frostbite in a few toes. Once at camp, the two took a break and warmed up. The pain prevented Susan from eating, but she was able to drink. They then struck camp, hiked back to the trailhead, and found a dentist.

ANALYSIS

The north ridge is the most popular technical climbing route on the Pfeifferhorn and is the cleanest option available, but is still fraught with detached granite blocks and unstable sections. Consequently, most parties attempt the route during the winter, when the rock is often frozen in. Given the low snowpack that winter, the route may have been looser than normal. It is possible that spontaneous rockfall occurred, but it seems most likely that Derek dislodged a rock when he tensioned the rope to belay Susan from above.

In this terrain, the team could have traveled without a rope or simul-climbed, but this would not eliminate the risk of rockfall or loose holds causing a serious fall. The best solution in such a scenario is likely traveling on a shortened rope for small distances (perhaps 10 or 15 feet at a time) and establishing quick but adequate belays for the follower, keeping in mind the danger of falling ice and rock when choosing a belay location. (*Source: Derek DeBruin.*)

FALL ON ROCK | Loose Rock, Descending Unroped
Little Cottonwood Canyon, Gate Buttress

On March 29, Emir Alikadic (38) and Thomas Gappmayer (27) had just finished climbing Tingey's Terror (5.7), a multi-pitch route on the Gate Buttress. After having lunch on top, the two decided to descend via a rappel into Green Adjective Gully, a popular cragging zone on the west side of Gate Buttess. The two traversed toward a set of anchors reached by a short, easy downclimb to a ledge. Just before Alikadic reached the ledge, the large flake he was holding for balance pulled out. He managed to push it out of the way of his chest and legs, but lost his balance and started tumbling backward. He desperately tried to grab rocks or trees as he fell, but to no avail. After falling approximately 50 feet, just before he went over the lip of the cliff, the rope he was carrying on his back in a mountaineer's coil snagged a feature on the rock and caught him.

Alikadic managed to grab a tree and pull into an alcove just below the lip of the cliff. This alcove contained anchors for the route Mother of Pearl (5.11+), which a party had just finished climbing, leaving a rope through the anchors. He assessed his injuries and found a swollen ankle, blood on the back of his head, loss of skin and bleeding on the hands and forearms, and broken fingernails from clawing at the rock as he fell. The rope suffered multiple core shots and the sheath was melted in several sections, even fusing two strands at one point.

Since Alikadic was conscious and felt he had full mental function, the two decided to self-rescue. Alikadic rappelled the rope set up on Mother of Pearl and got down into the gully, while Gappmayer descended with the help of another climber.

Alikadic was met by several others at the base of the cliff, one of whom happened to be an EMT. She assessed his injuries and suggested he wait for emergency services, but he decided to continue the descent unaided. The climber scrambled and hiked down to the parking lot, where he was met by police and EMTs, who released him after examining his injuries.

ANALYSIS

The fact that this incident didn't end in a fatality can largely be attributed to luck. The fall could have been mitigated or avoided by roping up for the easy yet semi-technical downclimb to the anchor. The flake that pulled out was identified by the victim and his partner as potentially unstable, mere moments before the accident. His instincts had warned him against touching it, and he had avoided stepping on it, but he didn't think it would dislodge with the minimal force he placed on it for balance. Whenever there is doubt about scrambling unroped over exposed terrain, or if low-quality rock is present, don't hesitate to belay a short section.

Alikadic was not wearing a helmet at the time of the accident. He and his partner had taken them off while having lunch, and he had never bothered to put it back on. (It was clipped on the back of his harness and was broken during the fall.) Though his head injury was fortunately only a minor laceration, it could have been avoided had he been wearing his helmet. Rappelling is a frequent cause of rockfall, as climbers move over the rock and maneuver the ropes. Keep the helmet on until safely out of any rockfall zone. (*Source: Emir Alikadic.*)

RAPPEL FAILURE | Inadequate Anchor, Piton Pulled Out
Canyonlands National Park, Monster Tower

On May 30, a 47-year-old man from Colorado was killed when his anchor failed while descending Monster Tower, above the White Rim in Canyonlands National Park. The victim, Climber A, was climbing with two companions, Climber B (27) and Climber C (15). The weather was hot, and in addition to their climbing gear all three carried daypacks with food, water, and extra clothing.

After some trial and error, the group found the base of the Kor Route (5.10 R), their intended climb for the day. The approach to the base of the route involves about 50 feet of 4th-class scrambling with a short section of easy 5th class. The three noted that this section, while easy on the way up, might be more difficult to downclimb with their packs at the end of the day. They opted to leave two of the packs above the scramble, at the start of the actual route, and climb the tower with one small pack. They anchored to an old piton at the base of the Kor Route, and Climber A began leading.

After climbing through pitch five, only Climber A wanted to continue to the summit, as the others were getting tired and thirsty. They considered rappelling, but didn't want to descend on the worn and aged anchors of the Kor Route, so after Climber A topped out, he lowered back to the other two climbers, and all three descended via the bolted anchors of the North Ridge Route. The three reached the saddle between Monster Tower and Washer Woman without incident and continued to the ground.

They still had to retrieve the packs at the base of the Kor Route. Climber A, followed by Climber B, hiked around the tower and scrambled up the approach again, planning to lower the packs off the old piton at the base and then either rappel or scramble back down. Climber A threaded the rope through the piton and set up a rappel as Climber B changed out of her climbing shoes. Climber A began rappelling, and then Climber B heard the sound of metal pulling out of the rock and a yell, and she saw that the piton and rope were gone. Climber C was screaming but didn't respond to questions from Climber B. Within about five minutes, Climber B had downclimbed the approach to Climber A, who was tangled in the climbing rope, with the old piton still attached. His skin was white. Climber B found no pulse or respiration. They had a cell phone signal, and Climber B told Climber C to call 911 while she began CPR. Climbers B and C performed CPR for the next hour while communicating with climbing rangers and the sheriff's department.

With daylight fading, the SAR team decided there wasn't enough light to deploy a helicopter and were forced to drive in to the basin. They reached the party at the base of the tower around midnight and helped Climbers B and C back to the vehicles, where they all camped for the night. The next morning, a helicopter was sent in to retrieve Climber A's remains.

Approaching the Kor Route on the east side of Monster Tower in Canyonlands. The piton anchor that failed was located at the base of the obvious chimney crack.

ANALYSIS

Though Monster Tower is remote, it receives regular ascents, and several climbers in an online forum attested to having recently rappelled off the same piton without incident. Nonetheless, antiquated fixed hardware, especially in the soft sandstone of the desert, should be thoroughly bounce-tested (with a backup) before committing to it. When rappelling off fixed gear, it's always prudent to back up the anchor with removable pieces when possible, until the last climber descends. And if there is any doubt about the integrity of a single piece of gear, leave a backup.

According to Climber B, the unexpected heat of the day and the resulting exhaustion and dehydration likely contributed to their decision-making, both in choosing to rappel instead of downclimb from the base of the climb, as well as to rappel off the piton without testing or backing it up. Carry plenty of water when climbing in the desert, especially during the hotter months. (*Source: Anonymous first-hand account.*)

Editor's note: Another incidence of fixed-anchor failure was reported at the end of November on the Turtle Wall, near St. George, Utah. A climber had finished a sport climb at the sandstone crag and clipped one of the two anchor bolts, moved a little higher, and then fell or let go. The bolt failed and he was caught by the highest protection bolt, hitting a ledge but fortunately without injury. The glue-in anchor bolt had pulled out of the rock when some of the soft sandstone around it blew out. This climber was fine because he was still on belay and clipped to protection, but it's a good reminder to always clip into both bolts at a sport anchor before untying to clean the anchor or rappel.

VERMONT

RAPPEL ERROR | Inadequate Equipment, No Backup
Green Peak, Bat Caves

On October 21, GR, a 45-year-old male from Vermont, and TW, a 43-year-old male, went to Green Peak near Dorset to climb in the Bat Caves area. They hiked to the top of a 40- to 50-foot cliff, where they used a static line to anchor themselves as they set up a top-rope anchored to a pair of bolts.

After completing the setup, the men decided to rappel the steep face rather than take the trail back to the base of the cliff. GR went first, even though he was the less experienced climber. He threaded their 7mm dynamic rope through his belay device, a Black Diamond ATC. His partner observed that the rope was too thin for the ATC, and suggested that GR add a second carabiner for additional friction, since he wasn't using a friction hitch or other backup. However, GR proceeded to rappel with a single carabiner connecting the ATC to his harness, and he started the rappel by jumping away from the cliff. As he dropped out of sight, TW heard him yell. Rather than rappel, TW descended the trail to the base and found his friend dead, with severe head trauma. GR was not wearing a helmet.

ANALYSIS

This accident was caused by improper use of equipment and inadequate rappel backup, which stripped GR of any ability to control his speed or stop his descent. Black Diamond recommends the ATC be used only with ropes that are 7.7mm or thicker (up to 11mm). As his friend suggested, GR could have clipped a second carabiner through the bights of the rappel ropes, adjacent to his main locking carabiner, creating additional friction in the system. He also could have employed a backup below the belay device by tying a friction hitch—a klemheist, Prusik, or autoblock—with a piece of accessory cord. Alternatively, he could have rappelled after his more experienced partner, who could have given GR a fireman's belay by tensioning the ropes from below to control his descent.

GR initiated the rappel by jumping out and away from the cliff, instead of proceeding slowly until he was confident that his rappel setup was adequate to control his speed. We do not know whether GR tested his setup while still safely anchored; if he had, he might have noticed the lack of friction in the system before untethering from the anchor. (*Source: Neil Van Dyke, Search & Rescue Coordinator, Vermont Department of Public Safety.*)

Before removing your anchor tether to lower, always check that the rope is threaded completely through the anchor and retied or clipped properly to your harness. *Ron Funderburke*

VIRGINIA

FALL ON ROCK | Failure To Retie Knot Before Lowering
Hidden Valley

On December 20, Jennifer Kendall "Kayah" Gaydish (36) fell from the anchors atop a sport route in the Ginseng area. An on-scene climber/paramedic and local EMS were unsuccessful in reviving her.

The route has a set of hangers with rings at the top. From what is known, the climber initially intended to rappel. She experienced some difficulty with the setup and decided to lower instead. While transitioning she hung from two daisy chains, pulled up a few feet of rope, tied a bight, and clipped it to her harness to prevent dropping the rope. (The bight was found attached to her harness when rescuers arrived.) She then untied the rope from her harness to thread it through the anchors in preparation for being lowered. It's at this point in the transition where no one really knows what happened. She called down to her belayer, asking to be put back on belay. She leaned back, her belayer felt some tension (which may have been the rope passing through the anchors), and then fell to the ground 50 to 60 feet below. She was still on belay when she fell, and no miscommunication was reported. (*Sources: Rock and Ice magazine, news reports, and local climbers.*)

ANALYSIS

It appears the climber did not close the system by tying the rope back into her harness after threading it through the anchor. Her decision to switch her descent plan from rappelling to lowering may have caused some confusion.

Whenever possible, climbers should leave their anchor tether(s) clipped while weighting the rope after retying through anchors, in order to test the system. If this is not possible, a careful visual check should be made before unclipping one's tethers. Going through a verbal checklist with the belayer may also be helpful. (*Source: The Editors.*)

Editor's note: A video tutorial demonstrating a good method for threading and cleaning a rappel anchor without going off belay can be found at americanalpineclub. org/best-practices.

The north side of Mt. Stuart, with the Ice Cliff Glacier, narrowing to a couloir near its top, left of the prominent north ridge. *John Scurlock*

WASHINGTON

FALL ON SNOW | Inadequate Protection
Mt. Stuart, Ice Cliff Glacier

About midnight on February 16, Eric Strickler, 29, and Edward McFarlin, 28, left their base camp at 6,500 feet and navigated the steep snow and ice walls of the Ice Cliff Glacier, past the bergschrund and into the final gully leading to the northeast shoulder. At 7:45 a.m., Strickler was belaying McFarlin up the last pitch of the gully, which was slightly corniced at the top. As he was climbing the cornice onto the ridge, a snow step collapsed beneath McFarlin and he fell, ripping out his only piece of protection, a picket placed just below the cornice. McFarlin rapidly slid toward his belayer, but Strickler was unable to arrest his fall. When their two-picket anchor failed, they fell another 800 to 1,000 feet onto the upper Ice Cliff Glacier.

Strickler was knocked unconscious in the fall, lost his helmet and pack, and was later diagnosed with three fractured vertebrae (C1, C4, and C5). McFarlin fractured his femur in two places. He managed to keep his backpack on, but the contents were strewn across the snow. After Strickler regained consciousness, the climbers found his personal locator beacon below them on the glacier and activated it. Their repeated attempts to call 911 were unsuccessful because of their remote location. While McFarlin assessed their situation, Strickler went to get his pack, which had an extra sleeping bag, food, and water. The climbers then insulated their sitting area and kept calling 911.

An hour later, a call connected to the Chelan County Sheriff's Office and dispatchers told them a ground team was being assembled. Eventually rescuers sent a helicopter and told the climbers to make themselves visible, which they did with space blankets and an orange sleeping bag. A rescuer lowered on a cable winch and strapped Strickler into a rescue harness before lifting him into the helicopter. The challenging terrain kept rescuers from being able to put McFarlin on a backboard to protect his fractured femur, but he was also lifted into the chopper. Both men were taken to Wenatchee Valley Hospital for treatment.

ANALYSIS

The climbers each had about half a dozen years of mountaineering and rock climbing experience but were new to technical alpine ice routes. After the incident, they acknowledged they would have been better off choosing a less demanding route or taking along somebody with more experience. With the semi-consolidated snow they encountered during the climb, they should have used horizontally buried pickets for anchors rather than vertically driving them in and clipping the top hole of the picket. Also, McFarlin was impatient to finish the last pitch and get out of the cold gully, so he climbed straight through challenging conditions on the cornice rather than stopping to establish a better anchor to protect the crux.

The two had packed well for an emergency, with extra layers, space blankets, lightweight sleeping bag, and personal locater beacon. In retrospect, they wished they also had put a stove in their summit pack. (*Source: Edward McFarlin.*)

Editor's note: In December, also in the Stuart Range, an experienced 33-year-old climber disappeared while attempting a solo ascent of the North Buttress Couloir on Colchuck Peak. The climber's tent was found at Colchuck Lake, but two days of ground searching and an aerial search by helicopter turned up no sign of him. Officials planned to search for evidence of the climber in the summer.

AVALANCHE
Granite Mountain

On the morning of December 31, American Alpine Club President Doug Walker, along with two friends, set out to climb Granite Mountain, west of Snoqualmie Pass. They planned to follow the winter route that avoids the active main avalanche chute on the south side of the mountain. This route skirts the hazard to the west and eventually gains a shoulder leading to the open summit slopes above. Near treeline, Walker's friends decided to turn back, and he continued to the summit solo. Late that afternoon, SAR resources were dispatched when he did not return to the parking lot. An advance team reached the summit lookout that night and reported no signs of Walker. Midmorning on New Year's Day, searchers followed a fresh avalanche path that ran below the summit slopes into the trees west of the line of ascent. Walker's body was found amid the debris, just below treeline.

ANALYSIS

Granite Mountain is a popular hiking and training destination for climbers, as it is very close to Seattle—Walker had climbed it countless times. The weather on December 31 was clear, sunny, and windy, with a freezing level at 1,000 feet. Other parties that day had noted wind slab forming on the steeper terrain near the summit. Familiarity with a mountain has many times affected the decision-making of even the most experienced climbers. Most of his friends were not surprised to hear that Doug wanted to tag the summit. He was very familiar with the hazards of winter snow travel, but this time they claimed his life. (*Source: The Editors.*)

FALL ON ROCK | No Anchor On Top
Dishman

Andrew Bower, 26, had taken it upon himself to replace worn bolts at this popular granite crag near Spokane with new stainless-steel gear. On November 6, he headed out alone to continue the project. His family went looking for him after he didn't return home that night and found his body at the base of the cliff.

Investigators found trampled moss and pine needles atop the cliff and believe Bower may have slipped as he approached the edge to fix a rope. He had not yet taken any gear out of his pack and was not wearing a harness. (*Source: News reports and Rock and Ice magazine.*)

ANALYSIS
There was a similar incident in 2015 when an unroped climber fell from the top of a cliff in Colorado. Especially in sport climbing areas, where the anchors usually are placed below the lip of the wall, the terrain at the top may be untraveled, loose, and slippery, and anchors can be difficult to reach from above. Placing a temporary anchor and tying in or rappelling to reach the main anchor would prevent most accidents like this one. (*Source: The Editors.*)

STRANDED | Exposure, Weather
Mt. Rainier

On June 11, Kyle Bufis, 25, and his partners, Derek Gavelis and Mathew Wiech, topped out on the challenging Liberty Ridge route on the north flank of the mountain. After reaching Liberty Cap, the trio got caught in high winds and whiteout conditions. They decided to hunker down in a crevasse near Liberty Saddle, the broad col at over 14,000 feet between Liberty Cap and Rainier's main summit, and wait out the storm. They soon realized they'd left their stove behind while resting earlier. Bufis offered to retrieve it and left the crevasse. He never returned. The other two climbers sent a text message asking for help, and on June 12, unable to find their partner, they downclimbed in high winds to Camp Schurman and met rangers there. Bufis' body was located the following day, "several hundred meters" from where he was last seen. (*Sources: Mt. Rainier National Park and news reports.*)

ANALYSIS
Although it was admirable to volunteer to retrieve the stove, Bufis and the team would have been better off remaining in the relative shelter of the crevasse until conditions and visibility improved. The exact circumstances of his fate are unknown, but it's likely Bufis simply got lost in the whiteout, in an area of the mountain with few landmarks, and succumbed to exposure. (*Source: The Editors.*)

RAPPEL ERROR | Inadequate Anchor, Failure To Check Knot
Mt. Rainier National Park, Sluiskin Mountain

On September 13, Timothy Hagan set out to finish the last of his climbs on the list of 100 Peaks at Mt. Rainier. The Chief is the eastern and highest peak of Sluiskin Mountain, a route that requires a 15-mile, 5,000-vertical-foot approach, followed by a blocky, 30-meter, 4th-class climb up an arête, with significant exposure. An

Sluiskin Mountain, with the Chief on the right. *Long Bach Nguyen*

average of six parties each year climb the route, both roped and unroped.

Hagan approached the peak with a non-climbing partner, who belayed him up the final 30-meter pitch, which he protected with two slings. He yelled to his belayer at the base of the climb that he didn't have webbing long enough to wrap around the large boulder commonly used as a rappel anchor. There were five interwoven loops of tied slings already wrapped around the boulder, but most were sun-bleached and worn. A new black sling was threaded through a steel rappel ring. Hagan chose to use this rappel anchor, but when he weighted the ropes, the webbing loop came untied and the ring slipped off the end. Hagan tumbled about 60 meters to his death.

A recovered photo of the sling before Hagan used it showed a knot concealed by a lip of rock; one end of this knot had a tail at least three feet long. Inspection of the webbing after the accident showed an overhand knot near one end and no knot on the other end. Rangers believe the overhand knot was the remnant of an incomplete or incorrectly tied water knot intended to join the webbing ends. Hagan may have felt enough friction from the long tail of webbing—either lying in the rocks or cinched inside the partially completed water knot—to be convinced the anchor was solid.

The anchor that failed had been left the previous day by another party. They had anchored their rappel through the steel ring and the black webbing but also threaded a strand of the existing, weathered webbing as their primary anchor, and they never weighted the newly placed backup sling.

ANALYSIS

Two possibilities can be considered for how the anchor failed. The party that set the anchor may have placed it correctly with a water knot, and Hagan untied it to adjust the position but didn't retie it. Or the first party didn't tie the anchor correctly but didn't realize this because the second piece of anchor webbing held their weight. Either way, Hagan failed to inspect his anchor adequately. Both Hagan and the previous day's party were at the anchor near dark and may have felt time pressure. Hagan's belayer said the climb took twice as long as anticipated and was cold and windy, so Hagan was likely tired and rushed. A second, redundant anchor likely would have prevented the accident. (*Source: Dan van der Elst, NPS Ranger.*)

Editor's note: According to Rainier National Park's annual mountaineering report, there were 55 search and rescue operations in fiscal-year 2015 (ending October 1, 2015), the busiest SAR year the park has ever seen, despite about a 9 percent drop in registered climbers. About 25 percent of emergency SAR incidents were attributed to climbers. There was one upper-mountain fatality (reported above), as well as three upper-mountain short-haul rescues.

WEST VIRGINIA

FALL ON ROCK | Darkness, Inadequate Protection
New River Gorge National River, Junkyard Wall

Four friends were climbing late at night on July 5 at the Junkyard Wall after bad weather earlier in the day delayed their start. Near 2 a.m., John (23) had just completed a solid lead of New Yosemite (5.9), using headlamps to light the way, but he was unhappy with his lead because he felt he had "stitched it up" with too much protection.

He then started up Four Sheets to the Wind (5.9+), placing multiple pieces of protection as he moved through the lower roof, including a solid piece at the lip. He headed up a corner to the upper roofs on the route, but rather than stop to place gear, as his belayer recommended, John continued into the upper roof crux and then fell. His tie-in was about nine feet above his last piece of gear, and he fell 22 feet before impacting the slab below the first roof. The climber immediately grabbed his right ankle and asked to be lowered.

John's partner splinted the ankle using shoes and climbing tape and, with the help of friends, evacuated the climber to their parked vehicle. The climber had a fractured right calcaneus (heel) that required surgical intervention and implantation of 15 screws. (*Source: Anonymous report from the climbers.*)

ANALYSIS
This incident occurred due to multiple factors, the most important being the limited visibility of a nighttime climb illuminated only by headlamps. This prevented an adequate assessment of the climb, potential gear placements, and fall zones. Without being able to see the slab below him, John may have mistakenly believed a fall would be safe because he had climbed around a roof. At the upper crux, he believed he did not have any pieces of the right size and chose to continue without adequate protection. To a lesser extent, pressure to climb within a limited time frame and his self-perception that he had overprotected the previous route were contributing factors. (*Sources: The climbers' report and the Editors.*)

FALL ON ROCK | Inadequate Protection, No Helmet
Summersville Lake, Coliseum

During the afternoon of July 31, a climber from Canada (name unknown) fell while leading Apollo Reed (5.13a) at Summersville Lake, a popular summer climbing area 30 minutes north of the New River Gorge National River. According to others present, the climber skipped the seventh bolt and was attempting to clip the eighth bolt when he fell. Due to the cumulative slack in the rope and at the belay, the climber struck the wall when he fell and then swung into a large boulder.

The climber landed headfirst on the boulder, striking just above his left eye. Witnesses called 911 and administered basic first aid. The climber remained conscious throughout the incident and was evacuated within 30 minutes by boat and then by helicopter to Charleston. Eyewitnesses reported the climber suffered multiple broken bones as well as unspecified head injuries. (*Source: Climbers at the scene.*)

ANALYSIS

This fall became serious primarily because of skipping available protection prior to reaching the crux of the route. Additionally, the climber was not wearing a helmet that could have prevented

A climber on Apollo Reed at Summersville Lake, high above the large boulders involved in an accident in 2015. *Mark Anderson*

or reduced the head injuries sustained from the fall. For information on how to identify and assess head injuries, see "Essentials: Head Injuries" in *Accidents 2015*. (*Source: R. Bryan Simon.*)

Editor's note: At least two other accidents that required medical attention occurred at Summersville Lake in 2015. Both were the result of leader falls on 5.8 climbs between Narcissus Wall and Orange Oswald Wall and resulted in ankle/lower leg injuries.

FALL ON ROCK | Failure To Clip Anchors
New River Gorge National River, Sandstonia

At 3 p.m. on November 6, a male climber (age unknown) fell while leading a sport route named Shady Lady (5.7) at the Sandstonia area of Bubba City. According to an NPS incident report, the climber was attempting to clip the anchors when he fell. Due to slack in the system, the climber fell approximately 15 to 20 feet before the belayer arrested the fall. The climber suffered injuries to his right buttocks and leg, in addition to facial injuries. (*Source: NPS Incident Report.*)

ANALYSIS

A combination of factors is likely the culprit for this long, painful fall, including fatigue and poor timing, with excessive slack pulled out to clip anchors. "Desperation" clips seldom work out well—either find a solid stance before pulling up slack or downclimb to the previous protection for a rest. (*Source: The Editors.*)

WISCONSIN

FALL ON ROCK | Inadequate Tie-in Knot, No Helmet
Devil's Lake State Park, Rainy Wednesday Tower

A father and his 9-year-old daughter were climbing at Rainy Wednesday Tower on September 19. The father had over 30 years of climbing experience, and the daughter had climbed indoors but did not have much outdoor experience. The father was standing on a ledge about 10 to 15 feet up the 50-foot face, and was either belaying the girl as she climbed or lowering her. The father said he had checked his daughter's gear and it appeared OK, but at some point she fell 10 to 20 feet to the bottom of the face and sustained multiple skull fractures.

Nearby climbers responded and provided first aid, maintaining her neck and spine position and keeping her airway clear. When the local fire rescue team arrived, they evacuated the patient by carrying her on a backboard up a steep access gully. She was airlifted to the hospital. (*Wisconsin Department of Natural Resources Visitor Accident Report and climber testimony.*)

ANALYSIS
The fall was not witnessed and the father was in shock and unable to provide details on what had happened, either at the scene or afterward. It appears that he was belaying from a stance partway up the cliff, perhaps to advise or encourage his daughter as she climbed or lowered. Various parties reported she was wearing a harness with an assortment of carabiners and "other gear" clipped to it, but the end of the climbing rope was not tied to her harness. The father was wearing a harness and his belay device was loaded with a strand of the same rope that was lying across the victim. The anchor at the top of the cliff appeared to be fine. It seems most likely the young climber's tie-in knot was improperly tied or unfinished. The girl was not wearing a helmet. (*Source: The Editors.*)

FALL ON ROCK | Inadequate Protection
Devil's Lake State Park, West Bluff

On November 8, a 23-year-old male climber was leading a pitch on the West Bluff, belayed from the ground by a friend. He had just set his second piece of protection, at approximately 25 to 30 feet, when he fell. The top piece pulled out, and the lower one failed as well. The lower piece was still placed in the rock, with a sling attached but no carabiner connecting it to the rope; the carabiner remained attached to the rope and fell to the ground with the climber. The victim fell approximately 25 feet and was unconscious for about 25 seconds. He indicated he had injuries to his right wrist and right hip and was concerned about a back injury. His helmet was scuffed and cracked. (*Wisconsin Department of Natural Resources Visitor Accident Report.*)

ANALYSIS
Inadequate protection was placed. The rock at Devil's Lake can be slippery and challenging to protect, and gear must be placed with extra care in the jagged rock, using slings and quickdraws for extension to keep protection from rotating out of

place. It's unclear if the lower piece was never clipped properly to the rope or if it became detached as the climber moved above it. Using a locking carabiner to clip a route's first piece of pro to the rope can provide some additional security.

This climber's helmet may prevented a much more significant injury. (*Source: The Editors.*)

Editor's note: Other climbing accidents at Devil's Lake in 2015 included a bouldering fall in which a 35-year-old woman broke her lower leg when her foot hit a rock before landing on the pads below the problem. There were several incidents of people falling while soloing or scrambling, but it's unclear if they were climbers or hikers.

WYOMING

AVALANCHE
Grand Teton National Park, Mt. Moran, Sickle Couloir

On May 17, four ski mountaineers were involved in an avalanche in the Sickle Couloir on the northeast face of Mt. Moran (12,605 feet). Three of the men were carried 500 to 600 vertical feet in the slide. They came to a stop on the surface, but one died at the scene as a result of injuries and a second died after being flown from the site by rescue helicopter. A third had lesser injuries.

The Sickle Couloir gains about 3,000 vertical feet and is given a mountaineering rating of Grade III 5.4. The four men in this incident were all very experienced ski mountaineers and were well equipped.

At 6:15 a.m., after crossing Jackson Lake by boat, the four men began their ascent to the Sickle Couloir Basin on foot. They did not encounter any snow until they arrived in the basin at approximately 7,500 feet. Here, they noted evidence of widespread wet avalanche debris that had been deposited sometime in the previous 24 hours. They discussed this observation and concluded that most of the significant recent snowfall would have been flushed from the Sickle Couloir, thus reducing the avalanche hazard. However, due to cloud cover, they were not able to see the conditions above 10,000 feet.

They continued upslope

The northeast face of Mt. Moran with the Sickle Couloir in center. The red dot marks the point where the avalanche struck a group of ski mountaineers, and the yellow dot shows where they came to a stop. *Rene Etter-Garrette*

on skis until they switched to crampons at the base of the couloir and began the actual climb unroped. The bed surface of the snow was very hard, with a thin, one- to two-centimeter layer of new snow lying on top. All four were climbing with a Whippet (self-arresting ski pole grip) in one hand and a normal ski pole in the other. After climbing approximately 600 feet, the group stopped for a short food and water break at an elevation near 9,900 feet. All four climbers were within five to six feet of each other.

The party heard potential avalanche activity above them. Seeing the oncoming snow, one of the surviving skiers moved slightly left and gripped the Whippet that he had forced into the firm snow. As the snow was hitting his right foot, he recalled the snow as being fairly slow-moving and relatively shallow (less than boot-top deep). He also felt that it took approximately two to three seconds for the snow to pass. After the snow had passed, he looked up to see that the others were gone.

The slide carried the other three through some narrow, very steep terrain where they most likely sustained their traumatic injuries while bouncing off the rock and firm snow. None of the three was buried for significant time during the event. The remaining skier descended immediately and began first aid. A call was made to 911 at 9:33 a.m. Continued snow sloughs forced him to move the most seriously injured skier to a safer location before help arrived. A large rescue effort ensued. Despite difficult flying conditions, all members of the party had been air-lifted from the scene by 2:30 p.m.

ANALYSIS

The Sickle Couloir is a committing climb and ski descent in the best of conditions. An unroped fall in the steep section of the couloir, either climbing or skiing, would likely be unstoppable.

In the preceding weeks, multiple storm systems had deposited new snow at the higher elevations in the Teton Range, with rain at the lower elevations. According to the Bridger Teton Avalanche Center's weekly snowpack summary, the most recent storm (May 7 to 9) had deposited a total of 21 inches of new snow, with over two inches of moisture, to higher elevations. Another storm system deposited 10 inches of new snow and an inch of water at the Rendezvous Bowl weather station during the period from May 15 to 16. While the party did experience light snowfall during their ascent of the couloir on May 17, the firm conditions in the couloir served to confirm their assumption that some snow had already slid and that the hazard was reduced.

The Sickle Couloir, and the terrain that feeds it, would concentrate any old or fresh snow that avalanched. While the avalanche that occurred was not large, it did entrain enough snow in the steep couloir to cause three of the four to fall.

A party's decision to go into the mountains is personal. Factors to be considered are the team's experience, abilities, fitness level, environmental conditions, and the acceptable level of risk exposure. Reports and evidence indicate the members of this team had the experience, ability, and fitness for the objective.

Fatal avalanche and/or ski mountaineering accidents seem to be on the rise in Grand Teton National Park. One to two of these events have been experienced each year for at least the past five years. Not only are these events traumatic for the parties and families involved, they can also expose rescuers to significant, if not extremely, hazardous conditions. While some amount of exposure is ever present in the mountains, mountaineers and rescuers alike must employ objective, prudent, and conservative judgment to minimize that exposure where possible. (*Source: National Park Service Search and Rescue Report.*)

ROCKFALL
Middle Teton, Dike Route

At around 8:30 a.m. on July 7, Pete Mumford, a past Grand Teton seasonal employee, heard rockfall and a subsequent call for help. He quickly made his way to the base of the Middle Teton, near the Black Dike, where he found Climber 2 tending to her husband, Climber

The Middle Teton (12,805 feet), with the Black Dike prominent in center and the South Fork of Garnet Canyon to the left. *NPS Photo*

1, who had a broken left humerus and severe lacerations. The two applied a tourniquet to control the bleeding. Mumfurd called for assistance at 9 a.m., and then helped the climbers move about 200 feet to get out of the rockfall hazard area.

Rangers were flown to a landing area below the accident site and quickly hiked up to the scene, arriving at 10:23 a.m. The team assessed the patient's vitals and injuries, administered pain medications, and applied an extremity vacuum splint and a C-A-T (combat application tourniquet) for uncontrolled bleeding. The patient was assisted in walking down to the helspot and transported to the hospital by helicopter and ambulance.

ANALYSIS
Climber 2 reported that she was belaying her husband up the initial pitch of the Dike Route when the accident happened. He was approximately 30 to 35 meters up the climb when a boulder estimated to be the size of five or six microwave ovens fell down the route and hit him. Despite his arm injury, Climber 1 was able to build an anchor with his uninjured arm, allowing the belayer to lower him to her location. Climber 2 was not hit by any of the debris.

This was a natural rockfall. Recent thunderstorms and rain showers may have loosened the matrix holding the rock in place, but it's unlikely the climbers could have foreseen the event. Both climbers (ages 27 and 29) were experienced, and they skillfully handled their initial self-rescue. (*Sources: National Park Service Search and Rescue Report and the Editors.*)

FALL ON SNOW | Loss Of Control While Glissading
Middle Teton, Southeast Couloir

At approximately 4:30 a.m. on July 25, Climber 1 and Climber 2 (both age 25) departed the Lupine Meadows Trailhead with plans to climb the Dike Route on the Middle Teton. At approximately 4 p.m. they reached the top of the Dike Pinnacle and decided, due to the time of day, not to continue to the summit.

They chose to descend to the South Fork of Garnet Canyon via the Southeast Couloir. After descending a few hundred feet, they encountered a snowpatch, which they decided to glissade. They were wearing helmets and had ice axes, and they both used a sitting glissading technique.

Climber 1 went first and glissaded out of Climber 2's view. Climber 2 didn't hear or see anything that indicated anything was amiss. Climber 2 then lost control during her glissade and slid approximately 100 to 200 feet before stopping at the bottom edge of the snowpatch. During the fall, she impacted a few rocks protruding from the snow and sustained minor injuries.

Climber 2 saw that Climber 1 had also slid out of control and tumbled off the snow and over rocky slabs, before stopping on a sloping grassy ledge. Climber 1 had slid and fell an estimated 200 feet. He was conscious but bleeding from wounds to his head. At approximately 5:20 p.m., Climber 2 used her cell phone to call for help.

Rangers were flown to an unimproved landing spot at about 11,200 feet, near the Ellingwood Couloir on the south side of the Middle Teton, and dropped off at approximately 7:25 p.m. The rangers scrambled over rocky terrain to reach the injured climbers 20 minutes later. After an assessment of both patients' condition, the technical nature of the terrain, and the time of day, the rescue team decided helicopter short-haul extraction of the two patients and the three rescuers would be the preferred method of rescue.

At approximately 8:40 p.m., Climber 1, with one ranger attending, was extracted from the grassy ledge. Climber 2 and two attending rangers were flown from the grassy ledge soon afterward and arrived at Lupine Meadows shortly after sunset.

ANALYSIS

In a telephone interview with a ranger the next day, Climber 2 said they should have avoided the snow and climbed down the adjacent rock slabs. Before committing to any glissade, it's prudent to test the snow surface in an area with no consequences in case of a slip. Be sure you know or can see the runout zone before glissading. Control your speed continuously with boot heels and ice axe, and don't hesitate to self-arrest aggressively if your speed grows too great. (*Source: National Park Service Search and Rescue Report and the Editors.*)

STRANDED | Off-Route
Middle Teton, Dike Route

On August 11, while attempting to climb the Dike Route on the Middle Teton, Climber 1 and Climber 2—brothers with 39 years of climbing experience in the Tetons—got off-route. Unable to locate the top of the Dike Pinnacle, a prominent feature of the route, the brothers began downclimbing and rappelling toward the South Fork of Garnet Canyon. Due to exhaustion and uncertainty about the terrain they encountered, the brothers requested a rescue.

At approximately 3:30 p.m., the brothers called the Jenny Lake Ranger Station and spoke to rangers, who made several attempts to direct them to easier terrain. These efforts failed, possibly due to the team's level of fatigue and fear.

Unsure of exactly where the pair was in relation to the lower Dike Route, and with concern for the party's mental and physical state, as well as continued requests for a rescue, rangers decided the best option was to either assist the pair by walking them off the mountain or to helicopter short-haul the pair to Lupine Meadows.

At 5:44 p.m. a helicopter left Lupine Meadows with three rangers onboard to conduct a reconnaissance. After a brief search, they located the pair on a large grassy ledge to the looker's left of the route. It was obvious that a rescue involving rangers climbing to the scene would be long and risky to the rescuers, so it was decided to mount a short-haul operation. Ranger Edmonds was short-hauled to the scene from Lupine Meadows. Edmonds placed both climbers in screamer suits, and the two were short-hauled to Lupine Meadows. The mission concluded at 8:40 p.m.

ANALYSIS

Although many climbers consider the Dike Route to be easy (5.5/5.6), those attempting it must remember that it is very long, with almost 3,000 vertical feet of climbing through complex terrain. Parties descending the route from points other than the sum-

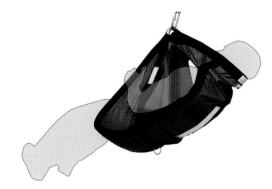

The Screamer Suit is often used to assist with helicopter evacuation of patients with no spinal injuries.

mit of the Middle Teton must be prepared for route-finding through loose rock that is much more challenging and complicated than the standard Middle Teton descent via the Southwest Couloir. Both climbers had researched the route in both guidebooks and online guides. They appeared to be well informed about the ascent route, but not well versed in their descent options, should they need to exit the route early. (*Source: National Park Service Search and Rescue Report.*)

STRANDED | Poor Position, Stuck Rappel Rope
Grand Teton, Stettner Couloir

On the night of August 15, at about 8:45 p.m., Teton Interagency Dispatch received a cell phone call stating that six persons were stranded in the Stettner Couloir. The subjects had climbed the Petzoldt Ridge and then rappelled into the couloir. They said that they rappelled through several waterfalls, were cold, and that their ropes were stuck. Due to the nature of the terrain and the onset of darkness, they were told that rescuers could not reach them until the next morning. The party was provided with strategies for both continued descent and for staying at their location and keeping warm.

At about 11:30 p.m., the incident commander recontacted the reporting party and learned that their group had joined forces with another party, and that they were now rappelling together. (The climbers were mostly in their 20s, with one group leader age 59.) The reporting party said she expected them to make it to the Lower Saddle that night, and two people did reach the Lower Saddle, where they were provided with sleeping bags for rewarming.

At about 5:45 a.m. on August 16, the incident commander received a text message from one of the party members stating that they were still stranded in the Stettner Couloir, that they were cold and wet, and that they needed rescue. Several rescuers climbed to the scene, and numerous others hiked and flew to the Lower Saddle to assist the subjects across the ledges at the base of the couloir. Eight people were evacuated out of the gully via rope rescue and escorted across the ledges to the Lower Saddle. Four of those individuals were flown from the Lower Saddle to Lupine Meadows because they were too incapacitated to hike out on their own.

ANALYSIS

Although many of the climbers involved had reasonable amounts of experience climbing in the Tetons, they started the ascent late—the party of six arrived at the base of the Petzoldt Ridge around 9 a.m. There were about ten people in front of them, including one group of four or five people. They were repeatedly delayed by the parties in front of them and arrived at the top of the Petzoldt Ridge—still far below the summit—at about 5 p.m.

Once on top of the ridge, the group decided they were not going to continue to the summit (via the Upper Exum Ridge) due to the time of day. They had a discussion about descending via Wall Street (the normal descent from this location), but decided that they were uncomfortable descending that route. However, rappelling the Stettner Couloir proved to be a poor option because of wet terrain, stuck rappel ropes, and exposure to rockfall. The climbers did not have the skills to ascend their stuck ropes to retrieve them, and after fixing their remaining rope and remants of two of the stuck ropes, they adopted unorthodox rappel techniques that could have proved disastrous (rappelling with two climbers on one single strand, one hanging from a tether beneath the other). Only two climbers were able to descend this way, leaving the others exposed to a cold night in wet clothing. When rappelling in lower-angle terrain with many obstacles, it's often better to do frequent shorter rappels, even if this requires building new anchors; full double-rope rappels greatly increase the risk of stuck ropes.

Researching the options for descent from a climb at various stages is as important as researching the ascent route. These climbers almost certainly would have been better off belaying each other across Wall Street and downclimbing the normal route to the Lower Saddle. (*Sources: National Park Service Search and Rescue Report and the Editors.*)

FALL ON ROCK, STRANDED | Off-Route, Inadequate Gear
Grand Teton National Park, Teewinot

At 7:30 a.m. on August 22, three women began hiking up the "Apex Trail" from the Lupine Meadows Trailhead in an attempt to climb Teewinot Mountain (12,325 feet). The three climbers, all in their mid-20s, were attempting to ascend the standard east face route, a route that Climber 2 had done once before. They were climbing in trail shoes and were not carrying a rope or harnesses, but each did have a helmet. The east face route is 4th class and is frequently climbed without ropes, but good route-finding skills and mountaineering experience are needed.

The women followed a well-established climbers' trail to a point level with the Worshipper and Idol rock towers. According to Climber 3, they stopped here, had a snack, and put their helmets on. Somewhere above this point and before the Narrows, they lost the main climbers' route and headed up to the north of the regular east face route. Believing they were now at the deep chimney adjacent to the Narrows, they climbed higher into steep, technical terrain at approximately 11,500 feet. They were now ascending a climb called the Black Chimney (5.6). They rock climbed several difficult pitches in their trail shoes.

After climbing around two or three large chockstones in the chimney, they were about 250 feet above the last big ledge. The women traversed left, across a narrow sloping ledge, and became increasingly certain that they were off-route. According to Climber 3, they had seen another climbing group below going a different way. The group discussed returning and going that way, but they were concerned about downclimbing what they had ascended.

According to Climber 3, she was on a small ledge to the right (north) of Climber 2. Climber 1 was trying to find a way up steep rock above Climber 2. Climber 1 fell about 10 to 15 feet and hit Climber 2, and Climber 3 watched the two bounce over the rocks multiple times, then disappear out of sight over the cliff. Climber 3 downclimbed 15 to 20 feet of easier terrain to a larger ledge. At approximately 11:15 a.m. she called 911. She yelled many times but could not get a response from her friends. Both the climbers who fell died from their injuries. Climber 3 was short-hauled by helicopter from the ledge at 4:19 p.m.

ANALYSIS

It's often easy to convince yourself that you're on-route, matching terrain features to guidebook descriptions or memory. Had the climbers recognized that the increased difficulty they encountered meant they were likely off-route, they might have stopped, retraced their steps, and returned to easier ground before it was too late. More appropriate footwear, with sticky rubber soles, might have given them more confidence to downclimb and retreat. It is also not uncommon to utilize ropes and rock protection to ascend and descend the normal route on Teewinot, when the rock is wet, icy, or when climbers feel uncomfortable with the exposure. (Sources: *National Park Service Search and Rescue Report and the Editors.*)

FALL ON SNOW | Inadequate Equipment, Poor Position
Middle Teton, Southwest Couloir

Climber 1 and Climber 2 had camped in Garnet Meadows on the night of August 28, with plans to climb the southwest couloir on the Middle Teton the following day. This route is 3rd class and is considered the easiest way to the summit. The two did not carry helmets, ice axes, crampons, ropes, or any other climbing gear. This equipment is not normally needed in late summer for a safe ascent of the peak, though helmets are often recommended because the route is popular and there is much loose rock in the couloir.

The two had a successful climb of the peak. On the descent, they found themselves at the top of a steep snow slope, north and east of the normal route, that often lingers all summer. They did not ascend this snow on their way up the peak earlier in the day. The snow on this slope is over 40° and has a bad run-out into the boulder field below it.

According to Climber 2, Climber 1 intentionally stepped out onto this steep snow, took one step, and immediately slid very fast down the length of the snowfield (about 100 feet) and then tumbled an additional 50 feet through the boulders. Climber 2 called for help around noon on August 29 and reported that Climber 1 (male, 22) was in and out of consciousness. Rangers responded by foot and helicopter, and the patient was short-hauled from the scene in a litter at 2:20 p.m.

ANALYSIS

When descending the same route that was climbed on the way up the mountain, it is usually a good idea to follow the same line, provided the terrain was reasonable to ascend and fit the route description. The snowfield where Climber 1 lost his footing appears to offer a tempting shortcut back down into Garnet Canyon's South Fork, and this is why numerous accidents have occurred here. The snow in late summer is very firm, and even a climber well versed in the use of an ice axe would be challenged to self-arrest a fall on this slope. These climbers had no axes. (*Sources: National Park Service Search and Rescue Report and the Editors.*)

ANCHOR FAILURE | Off-Route
Wind River Range, Pingora Peak

On August 28, Sublette County sheriff's dispatch center received a satellite telephone call from a backpacker in the Cirque of the Towers. The caller had witnessed two climbers fall from the northeast face of Pingora (IV 5.8+).

Tip Top Search and Rescue responded directly to the scene with Sublette County's contract heli-

The northeast face of Pingora begins with a long traversing pitch. When two climbers tried to avoid retreating across this traverse and instead rappel straight down the face, they fell to the ground after an anchor failed. *Rex Headd*

copter. Pilot Mario Nickl and volunteers Tony Chambers and Shawn Streeter were able to locate the backpacker, along with the two fallen climbers at the base of the northeast face. The helicopter landed at Lonesome Lake and then returned for two more rescuers, volunteers Milford Lockwood and Andrew Masters. Tony and Shawn hiked the short distance to the scene and found the two climbers, Jonathan Peter MacDonald (23) of Lander and Keith Murray Hendersen (57) of Cheyenne, deceased from their fall.

The evidence found at the scene showed that Keith had Jonathan on belay with about 30 feet of rope in service. Jonathan was tied in to the rope with a figure 8, which was found tight as if from a fall. Keith had the rope through a belay device but was not tied in to the other end of the rope. He was clipped into a piece of webbing and a piece of cordelette, both of which were badly faded and frayed, and which appeared to be the remnants of an old rappel anchor. He was clipped to the old anchor using a single sling with non-locking carabiners. There was no other gear placed between the two climbers. Both climbers were wearing helmets, but Jonathan's had come off during the fall. The reporting party stated he had seen the two climbers descending before their fall.

A few days later, Tip Top Search and Rescue received a phone call from a separate pair of climbers, Reuben and Breezy, who had encountered Keith and Jonathan earlier that day on the northeast face. Reuben stated that they caught up to Keith and Jonathan after the first pitch, which is a traverse. Jonathan and Keith were moving very slowly, and offered to let Reuben and Breezy pass, which they declined. Reuben stated they waited about 45 minutes while Jonathan and Keith climbed the second pitch. Reuben led closely behind the others and then set up a belay some distance above them. Reuben recalled hearing the two discussing that they had underestimated the difficulty of the climb, that it was getting late already, and that they should retreat.

Reuben and Breezy pushed on and later recalled that Keith and Jonathan rappelled down the second pitch but elected not to traverse back along the first pitch. Instead, they continued to rappel straight down the steep slabs below. Reuben stated he saw one of the climbers walking around on a ledge, looking for a way down. Reuben and Breezy had no other contact with the pair but heard them yell "Rock" at one point. They had no idea anything was wrong until they saw the helicopter respond to the base of the climb.

ANALYSIS

While it is impossible to know exactly what happened to Keith and Jonathan, two different parties saw them descending before the accident. It appears that Keith had put Jonathan on belay to downclimb, traverse, or climb back up toward the route line. One or both of them fell, and the old rappel anchor to which Keith was clipped then failed. Though both of the anchor slings were badly faded and frayed, they were found still intact, which would lead one to believe that either the rock horn holding the slings failed or the old slings came off the top of the horn. Lessons from this incident include:

- Back up or replace faded or tattered slings and cordage at anchors
- Test natural rock anchors (horns, chockstones, etc.) by pushing, pulling, and knocking on the rock, with a backup if possible
- Research escape routes before a big climb and observe anchors and other "bail" options as you climb
- Use locking carabiners for anchor tethers
- Make sure the chinstrap on a helmet is fastened snugly and securely

(*Source: Tony Chambers, Tip Top Search and Rescue.*)

Editor's note: Search "Twin Peaks" at publications.americanalpineclub.org for another reported accident in the Wind Rivers in 2015.

CANADA

Unless otherwise noted, reports in this section were drawn from park reports and summaries, and Robert Chisnall of the Alpine Club of Canada provided the analyses.

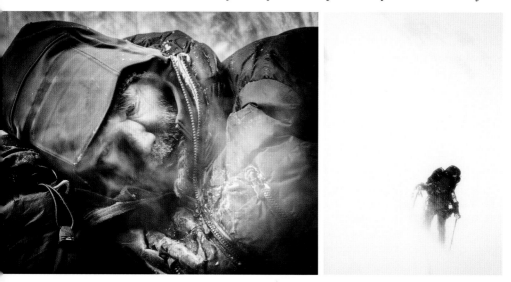

A severe storm caught three climbers high on Mt. Logan and led to frostbite, hypothermia, and symptoms of high-altitude pulmonary edema. The three climbers spent 12 days over 5,000 meters (16,400 feet) before calling for a rescue, and another two days before a helicopter could reach them. *Bryce Brown*

STRANDED | Severe Weather
Yukon, Kluane National Park, Mt. Logan

A group of three experienced mountaineers climbed the east ridge of Mt. Logan, starting on May 16, with the plan of traversing the summit plateau and skiing down the normal route (King Trench). They had excellent weather and generally good conditions during the ascent, and they summited on June 2.

The next day the weather changed and an intense storm hit the team high on the mountain. In order to reach their planned descent, the team needed to climb over a col between the east and main summits, at an altitude of approximately 5,700 meters. During the traverse over the col in the storm, one member sustained frostbite to both hands and became hypothermic. The team dug into a crevasse on the col, where the climbers were pinned down for three days by intense wind (estimated 160 kph) and an estimated two meters of snowfall.

During a one-day break in the weather, the team traversed the plateau toward King Trench but could not make it all the way across. Another four days of marginal weather followed. The team was unable to travel and risked refreezing the frostbitten hands. Food and fuel supplies began to dwindle. A second climber began experiencing intermittent symptoms of high-altitude pulmonary edema (HAPE). The team's low energy after 12 days of being at an altitude of more than 5,000 meters, the frostbitten hands, and HAPE symptoms made them increasingly concerned that they would not be able to safely reach the bottom of Kings Trench and a pre-placed cache with their remaining supplies. On June 9, they called Parks Canada to request assistance.

The altitude and terrain at their location was at the upper limit for a helicopter rescue. A powerful A-Star B3 helicopter from Trans North helicopters was brought in for the job, and a second A-Star B3 with rescuers from Denali National Park was brought in as backup. A team from Banff National Park trained in technical mountain rescue was put on standby and helped with logistics.

On June 11, a break in the weather occurred and a Visitor Safety team from Kluane National Park was able to fly into the area and extract all three climbers, flying them back to Haines Junction. Three landings were required at 5,300 meters on a glaciated plateau, with no options for escape if the weather moved in. The pilot and rescue team pulled it off smoothly.

ANALYSIS

The summit plateau of Mt. Logan is an extreme place to be caught by severe weather. In order to descend the Kings Trench, climbers need to ascend 300 vertical meters to Prospector Col. A solid weather forecast, good fitness and acclimatization, good gear, and a bit of luck are essential for a safe descent off the mountain. Sometimes these conditions align, but sometimes they do not.

This climbing team was well equipped and experienced, but they were unlucky to get some fierce weather. Fortunately they had good equipment and knowledge of how to survive in such a hostile environment. Additionally, they had communication devices to call for help and some food reserves to wait out an extended storm. One of the participants said, "We used a SPOT and a satellite phone for communications. The sat phone was indispensable during the rescue coordination. We could not have arranged it all with one-way comms."

FALL ON SNOW | Inadequate Protection
British Columbia, Joffre Peak

On January 11, three climbers perished after falling nearly the full length of the Central Couloir on the north side of Joffre Peak, east of Pemberton. The couloir is best known as an extreme ski descent, but this trio was ascending the route as a snow and ice climb. They were climbing roped and had neared the top of the route when something caused one or more of them to fall, pulling all three into a fall of about 600 meters. When the climbers did not rendezvous with friends and family as planned, they began a search and discovered the fallen climbers at the foot of the peak that night. (*Source: News reports.*)

ANALYSIS

The climbers (ranging in age from late 20s to 30s) were experienced and well equipped. It is not possible to say exactly what caused them to fall, but investigators reported there was no avalanche debris at the base of the route. It appears most likely that one climber fell with either inadequate protection or anchor (or both) and pulled the others off. (*Source: The Editors.*)

FALL ON ROCK | Inadequate Protection
British Columbia, Squamish, The Apron

For the first route of our first day of climbing in Squamish, my climbing partner and I started up Calculus Direct, a 5.9 variation start to Calculus Crack on the Apron. I led the first pitch (5.9) with ease, built an anchor, and brought up my second. Starting the second pitch (5.8), I traversed a few feet along a sloping ledge, placed a cam, and then started up a vertical hand crack. After climbing above my initial piece of protection, I decided to make one more move before placing another piece. I awkwardly attempted to toe jam into an adjacent crack and released my solid hand jam for what I thought would be a good hold higher up. However, the hold was not there, and I ended up losing my balance and falling onto the ledge below. I broke my right ankle, fracturing bones in four places, and continued falling until the cam caught my fall.

A climber making the crack switch on pitch two of Calculus Crack. *Steph Abegg*

My partner, Charles Cooper, secured me to the anchor and removed me from the belay, then attached his Grigri to the master point and lowered me without incident. I was able to reach the nearby road with assistance from some awesome climbers on the trail. I was taken to the emergency room in Squamish, where they attempted unsuccessfully to reduce a dislocation, and eventually we drove to Vancouver, where I received ankle surgery.

ANALYSIS

This injury was entirely avoidable. I was ascending a great set of hand cracks, which provided ample opportunities for protection. I had become comfortable with runouts over moderate terrain and did not feel the 5.8 grade was anything to worry about. I consciously chose not to place an additional piece of protection, even though a fall would inevitably result in striking the ledge. This decision was partly out of a desire to save gear for the remainder of the pitch, but also was borne out of my belief that I would not fall from a 5.8 hand crack.

I have been climbing for five years and trad climbing for about three years, and I broke several of my personal climbing rules that morning. Most prominently, I failed to respect the fact that a fall can happen even when you think a climb is well within your ability. (*Source: Tyler Lobdell.*)

FALL ON ROCK | Inadequate Belay, No Helmet
British Columbia, Skaha, Foreplay Wall

On June 7, a 38-year-old climber was leading a well-bolted 5.10a route on Foreplay Wall. It was midafternoon on a hot day, and the 30-meter cliff was just coming into the sun. The belayer (age about 42), with whom the leader had climbed "many times before," had returned to climbing after a two-year absence due to injury. It was reported that the belayer had three years of experience and the leader had 15 years of experience. The climbers had borrowed a brand-new rope from another climber at the crag—a 9.5mm rope with a water-resistant sheath. The rope's owner had said it was slick on rappel, and had recently bought a new device to provide more friction. The belayer was using a standard Black Diamond ATC belay device.

The leader reported that he climbed the route quickly and easily. He arrived at the last bolt and either unexpectedly slipped or a hold broke. The belayer lost control of the rope and was unable to arrest the fall. The leader fell about 20 meters to the base of the climb.

The climber landed on angled ground, which launched him face-first into some rocks farther down the slope. The impacts resulted in a broken right calcaneus—his shoe was split, and so was his heel to the bone—and a deep left-heel laceration. Multiple frontal facial lacerations were sustained, including a torn right nostril, and he had head trauma and a concussion. After two hours, the injured climber was evacuated by helicopter. He spent six days in an intensive-care unit.

ANALYSIS

Several factors were identified by the climbers. The leader was climbing fast because the route was easy for him, and the climbers were in a hurry to leave the crag now that it was coming into the sun. There may have been excess slack in the rope when the leader slipped. The belayer was not located in an ideal position, close to the wall, and when the rope came tight as the leader fell, the belayer tripped, compromising his braking position. Consequently, the belayer was unable to stop the rope running through the device and his hands were burned.

Climbers must be cautious when using thin or new ropes, which tend to be more "slippery" than ropes that have seen some use. The use of a tube-style or assisted-braking belay device specifically designed for thinner ropes might have helped. Belay gloves also can help with controlling a severe fall. Fundamentally, however, a good belay stance and position, combined with proper braking technique (brake hand held firmly on the rope below the belay device, ready for a fall), are the keys to preventing such accidents.

The leader typically wore a helmet when climbing, but elected not to wear it on that climb because of the heat (about 35°C/95°F). He observed that the helmet "wouldn't have provided much facial protection," but it might have helped with his other head injuries. "I know am very lucky to come out without worse injuries, but I have for sure used up one of the nine lives," he said. (*Source: The Editors, with anonymous leader's report, compiled using statements from the belayer and other climbers at the crag.*)

FALLING ICE | Poor Position
Alberta, Ghost River Valley

On February 2, a party of two was ascending a four-pitch WI5 ice route called Sorcerer. Low on the route, one of the climbers was struck by falling ice. He was lowered to the ground and a rescue was requested using a SPOT device. A multi-agency rescue ensued. The injured climber was treated for head and neck injuries and then flown out to the Ghost River Ranger Station. The injured climber had sustained a concussion and a sprain (location not specified).

ANALYSIS
Rescue personnel concluded that the evacuated climbers had been in a poor position on the route. Scarcity bias may have been at play–multiple parties had converged on this remote and coveted route that day, after approaching for several hours. The individual reporting the accident speculated that there was not much communication among the parties and that language barriers were possible contributory factors.

Climbing underneath other ice climbers profoundly increases one's exposure to falling ice. If you insist on climbing beneath other climbers, try to climb on the opposite side of the route, relative to the party or parties above. Establish belay stances in protected locations.

AVALANCHE | Poor Position
Alberta, Banff National Park, Polar Circus

At 5:30 a.m. on February 5, two climbers set out to climb Polar Circus, a 700-meter ice climb on Mt. Cirrus. It had snowed lightly overnight and continued to snow during the day. Later in the afternoon, they observed snow sloughing off the steep cliffs adjacent to the climb. The climbers reached the top at 4 p.m. and began rappelling the route.

Just before dark the climbers reached a large snow slope in the middle of the climb. The first climber began walking across the snow to set up the next rappel station while the second climber coiled the ropes and put on his headlamp. At 6 p.m. the second climber reached the middle of the snow slope and observed his partner's tracks disappearing into a fresh avalanche fracture line. The avalanche debris was spread out over the next two pitches of the ice climb, a distance of approximately 200 meters.

The second climber rappelled down and spent two hours doing a visual search and probing likely spots in the avalanche debris with his climbing gear, but was unable to locate his partner. As the incoming storm intensified, he wisely decided to continue rappelling and arrived at his car at 11 p.m. At 11:30 p.m. he contacted the Parks Canada Visitor Safety team via satellite phone from a nearby hostel to request assistance.

A Parks Canada team flew in to the site the next morning to do an aerial search but was unable to locate any signs of the missing climber. As the storm continued, the avalanche hazard increased and the recovery effort was delayed several days until avalanche control was completed on the slopes above the accident site.

On February 9, search teams were inserted into the accident site by helicop-

A climber beneath the final pitches of Polar Circus. Fresh snow can make this long route hazardous, with numerous avalanche terrain traps. *John Price*

ter long line, and a search began with dogs, a RECCO search device, and probing of likely burial spots in the debris. On February 10, a faint RECCO signal was found near some weak dog indications (even though the climbers had not been equipped with RECCO reflectors), and on February 11, a probe strike near this spot located the missing climber under 2.8 meters of snow. It was later determined that the climber had died as a result of trauma sustained in the avalanche, and that the faint RECCO signal was reflected off a headlamp in his pack.

ANALYSIS

The primary issue was a failure to recognize the increasing avalanche hazard throughout the day. Given the large amount of avalanche terrain above this climb, the confined nature of the climb, and the steepness of the snow slope midclimb, small changes in weather can rapidly increase the avalanche hazard on this route.

The avalanche bulletins for the region had rated the alpine and treeline hazard as Moderate to Low, but indicated that the arrival of an incoming storm would create a substantial rise in the avalanche hazard. The storm arrived earlier than forecasted, with new snow accumulations of 10 to 12 centimeters during the day, increasing winds, and warming temperatures. These changes caused hazardous snow conditions. The first climber either triggered the steep snow slope he was crossing or got hit by an avalanche from above while crossing the slope. Diligently monitoring conditions, watching for clues such as sloughing, and being willing to turn back when changes occur are critical when traveling in steep, confined avalanche terrain.

While many ice climbers choose to climb in avalanche terrain without carrying avalanche rescue gear, this trend is beginning to change. In this case, avalanche gear would not have prevented the climber from dying, but it would have reduced the time his partner spent searching for him under increasingly hazardous conditions. For the rescue teams, this would have significantly reduced the duration of their exposure to the avalanche slopes above the climb. Wearing gear with sewn-in RECCO reflectors also can substantially assist a rescue team.

Editor's note: A solo climber died in an avalanche from a snowfield on Polar Circus in 1982. In November 2015, five climbers were caught in an avalanche on the north side of Mt. Stanley in Kootenay National Park and were carried about 60 meters downslope. Fortunately, they were able to dig themselves out and were not seriously hurt.

FALL ON ROCK | Loose Rock
Alberta, Bow Valley Wildland Provincial Park, Ha Ling Peak Boulders

A female climber in her 20s was bouldering at the base of Ha Ling Peak, near Canmore, on March 27. A piece of the boulder detached and crushed her pelvis. She was evacuated from the scene utilizing a wheeled stretcher.

ANALYSIS
The climber failed to test her holds. Much of the Canadian Rockies is soft limestone, which is susceptible to frost jacking during the seasonal freeze-thaw process. This is true whether you're climbing alpine walls or the boulders at their base.

RAPPEL FAILURE | Miscommunication, No Stopper Knots
Alberta, Bow Valley Wildland Provincial Park, Cougar Creek Canyon

On April 28, two climbers were descending a single-pitch route known as Aces High on Casino Wall. One of the climbers rappelled off the ends of the rope. He fell about five meters and landed on his back, sustaining a lower back injury described as a fracture, and had to be evacuated.

ANALYSIS
This accident was attributed to inadequate communication and a failure to double check the length of the route relative to the length of the rope. The guidebook notes the climb is 31 meters high, making it very difficult to rappel safely with a single 60-meter rope. Tying stopper knots in the ends of the rope before rappelling could have prevented the climber from hitting the ground.

FALL ON ROCK | Off-Route
Alberta, Banff National Park, Castle Mountain

On July 24, Banff Dispatch was relayed a 911 call from a climber whose partner had just taken a 15-meter leader fall on the upper cliffs of Castle Mountain. They indicated they were at the bottom of a popular route, Brewer Buttress (III 5.6), on the Goat Plateau, a wide band of scree midway up the mountain. The lead climber had hit his head, had back pain, and was unable to move on his own but was conscious.

A crew of three Visitor Safety (VS) specialists from Banff and a mountain rescue pilot flew to the scene. After searching the base of Brewer Buttress with the helicopter and not finding any sign, it was discovered that the two climbers were in fact 250 meters left of that route on an unknown or unclimbed line. One VS specialist was inserted close to the wall via a hover exit, and then the helicopter landed at a staging area on the Goat Plateau.

Once more details were acquired, the remaining two VS specialists, with medical gear, were heli-slung close to the scene. The wall above the patient was too steep to heli-sling directly, so the rescue team lowered the patient in a stretcher to a rudimentary trail 50 meters below. Once there, the patient was packaged and heli-slung directly to a waiting ambulance.

ANALYSIS
The largest contributor to this accident was the climbers convincing themselves that the terrain matched the description they had read for a popular climb. How-

ever, they ended up climbing terrain more difficult than their intended 5.6 route, along with loose rock with marginal natural protection. Along with carrying a written guidebook description and a photo of the route if available, it is very helpful to landmark large features from various vantages before and during the climb. Getting advice from those who have experience with a particular route is also helpful.

Castle Mountain. Arrow marks the approximate location of Brewer Buttress, above the Goat Plateau ledge.

FALL ON ROCK |
Scrambling Alone
Alberta, Banff National Park, Mt. Whyte

Late in the afternoon of July 28, a lone 30-year-old male was traversing the exposed alpine rock ridge heading southwest from the summit of Mt. Whyte toward Popes Peak. Partway across this traverse, the subject dislodged some loose rocks and fell approximately 300 meters down the northwest side of the ridge, coming to a rest on a flat bench below the face on the upper extent of the Divide Glacier. This face consists of an icy gully with rock bands, with an overall angle of about 45°. The patient was unable to move and lay in the snow calling for help.

At 7:30 p.m., Parks Canada received a call from a party of three scramblers descending the nearby summit of Mt. Niblock. They reported cries for help from an unidentified location. Parks Canada responded with two rescuers and a helicopter and began searching the area. At 8:15 p.m. the patient was located, and rescuers were able to land at his location.

The patient suffered spinal trauma and was paralyzed from the chest down, and he was approaching a hypothermic condition. The patient was immobilized with spinal precautions and loaded directly into the helicopter.

ANALYSIS
Climbing alone always presents serious risks, including falling unroped and lacking a partner to provide assistance in case of an incident. Given the seriousness of his injury, this patient was fortunate that other parties were nearby and able to hear his cries for help. It is unlikely he would have survived the night outside. The reporting party certainly saved his life.

This situation is a good reminder to always leave a detailed trip plan with someone at home, and to carry communication devices to call for help if possible.

Editor's note: A report about another serious scrambling accident in 2015, on Mt. Daly in Yoho National Park, can be found at publications.americanalpineclub.org. Search "Mt. Daly."

ROCKFALL

Alberta, Canmore, Grassi Lakes

Two people were injured on August 1 by rockfall at the crag known as the Golf Course. The two had just arrived at the crag and were gearing up, and had not yet put on their helmets. Shoebox-size rocks came down, striking the two individuals. One was briefly knocked unconscious and had a severe head laceration. The second climber had a large goosebump on her head. The first patient was carried down to a vehicle on the easy access trail and subsequently transported to emergency medical services at the trailhead.

ANALYSIS

This area is known for rockfall hazard from the steep, sloping ground above the cliff, often knocked off by tourist visitors or mountain goats. Nonetheless, these sport climbing crags are very popular. To mitigate the risks, don a helmet before reaching the base of a cliff prone to rockfall, and when possible seek sheltered areas for belaying or hanging out between climbs.

FALL ON ROCK

British Columbia, Yoho National Park, Chancellor Peak

On August 7, a pair of climbers set out to attempt a new route on the north face of Chancellor Peak. After climbing a considerable distance, they encountered poor conditions and decided to traverse to the northwest ridge to complete their ascent. As the lead climber was gaining the ridge, a hold broke and he fell 10 to 15 meters, sustaining injuries to his knee and a large laceration on his leg. The pair was able to move over to a small ledge where they used their first-aid skills to close the wound and stop the bleeding. However, they realized they would not be able to continue climbing, and they used their cell phone to call for a rescue.

At 8:37 p.m., Banff Dispatch received the call. After confirming the location of the climbers and determining there was enough daylight left to attempt to reach them, two Visitor Safety staff members flew out to the accident location with Alpine Helicopters Inc. The two climbers were located on a small ledge at an altitude of approximately 2,900 meters, and a staging area was set up at the Chancellor-Vaux Col (2,580 meters). Using a line below the helicopter, a Visitor Safety member was slung onto

Location of an accident and rescue on the northwest ridge of Chancellor Peak. *Parks Canada*

the ledge next to the climbers. The two climbers were then slung out to the Chancellor-Vaux Col, loaded into the helicopter, and flown to Lake Louise just before dark.

ANALYSIS

This accident took place in steep terrain near the end of the day. The fact that the injuries were relatively minor and that the climbers were rescued that night is largely a result of the preparedness and prompt actions of the climbing team.

The reporting person had a cell phone with good service and was able to provide Banff Dispatch with a very good description of their location and injuries. This good two-way communication also allowed Banff Dispatch to advise the climbers on how to get organized for the rescue, which helped the Visitor Safety team complete the mission before dark.

During the fall, the climber was flipped upside-down and fell headfirst. Fortunately, he was wearing a helmet. He stated that his helmet took several major impacts, but he did not sustain any head injuries.

The team had substantial knowledge of first aid and was able to assess and care for the injuries prior to the arrival of the Visitor Safety team. The climbers were also able to move to a safer and more accessible location and wait for help. These steps allowed for a very efficient rescue.

Finally, the team had enough equipment to spend the night outside, had this been required. This gear helped them stay warm while they waited for the arrival of the Visitor Safety team.

ROCKFALL | Near Miss With Rockslide
Alberta, Banff National Park, Grand Sentinel from Moraine Lake

On August 15, 2014, Will Richardson-Little and I started hiking toward the Grand Sentinel at 7:20 a.m. from the Moraine Lake parking lot. Our objective was to climb the normal route on the south face (4 pitches, 5.9). We had a standard rack, double ropes, and helmets.

We reached Sentinel Pass about two hours later and started our descent toward the Sentinel. Following the guidebook description, we scrambled along the scree slopes on the left side of the valley (the same side as the Sentinel). The rock was loose and unsettled. A rock the size of a tennis ball fell past me, and I should have taken this as a sign. It had rained lightly the day before.

It took about 30 to 45 minutes to cross the scree

The climbers' shortcut from Sentinel Pass to the Grand Sentinel is exposed to rockfall from Pinnacle Mountain. *Eric Chow*

slope to reach the Sentinel. After we'd completed the first pitch, between 10 a.m. and 11 a.m., we heard the sound of falling rock. A significant rockslide, lasting five minutes, occurred on the scree slopes we had just crossed, not half an hour earlier. The rockslide was 50 to 100 meters wide. Large boulders, the size of milk crates or possibly larger, were hurtling down with alarming force. The thunder, cracks, and rumbles of the slide could be heard across the valley. After the rockslide, my partner and I realized that we were very lucky. If we had been caught in that area, with nowhere to take cover, we both surely would have been killed.

ANALYSIS

The slide was likely due to warming temperatures in the late morning and melting snowpack high on Pinnacle Mountain, above the traverse. These conditions likely caused a large boulder or boulders to be released from the snow. The subsequent fall of these large rocks initiated a full rockslide. Scattered rockfall continued throughout the day.

We completed the standard route on the Grand Sentinel (an excellent climb) and descended directly downhill from the Sentinel and across the valley to return by the hikers' trail. Our alternative route was on the opposite side of the scree slopes, adding about 15 minutes to the hike out.

Red dot shows the approximate location where two ice climbers surprised a grizzly bear in the dark while descending from the base of Dirty Love, a very difficult climb on the west side of Mt. Wilson. *Raphael Slawinski*

This near miss taught us a good lesson about being aware of objective hazards. When the day's goal is a rock climb, it can be easy to get shortsighted and forget that there are other, bigger hazards all around. In the alpine environment, it's smart to get a very early start, even for a short rock climb. (*Source: Eric Chow.*)

BEAR ATTACK
Alberta, Banff National Park, Mt. Wilson

On November 29, British climbers Greg Boswell and Nick Bullock were descending in the dark from a reconnaissance of a very difficult mixed route high on the west side of Mt. Wilson, above the Icefields Parkway, when a grizzly bear attacked Boswell, badly biting one of his legs. Boswell fought back until the bear dropped him. The two retreated as quickly as they could, but not as quickly as they would have liked because of darkness and technical terrain (including rappels). Upon reaching the hospital early the next morning, Boswell required numerous stitches for his wounds.

ANALYSIS

This incident was widely reported and more details can be found online, including a first-person account on Bullock's blog (*nickbull-*

ock-climber.co.uk). Wildlife officials said the climbers likely stumbled on the bear's den as it was preparing to enter hibernation. Parks Canada closed the area for the remainder of the winter to protect the bear. Grizzly bears may not go into hibernation until ice season is well under way in the Canadian Rockies. Climbers should consider carrying bear spray as a precaution, at least during approaches. (*Source: The Editors.*)

FALL ON ROCK | Incomplete Tie-In Knot
Québec, Racine, Lac Larouche

On September 17, two female climbers in their 20s were top-roping a 5.10c route called Gueuse. One climber had just completed the route. The sun was going to set in 20 to 30 minutes. Everyone else at the crag had just left, so the two climbers were alone.

The climber reported the incident as follows: "I completed my figure 8 knot, but at the exit of the knot I didn't leave enough rope. I left only 1.5 to 2 inches of rope. I really didn't feel like redoing my knot and had done this [in the] past with no issue. And I just started climbing without performing a partner check."

While exiting an overhang, her hand slipped. "I fell away from the wall as the rope took my weight and slowed me down for a fraction of a second. The knot had come undone [and] I was falling toward the ground."

The climber landed feet-first and ended up with a fractured calcaneus in her left foot and a laceration on her right leg that needed five stitches. The belayer helped the injured climber to hop from the forest back to the parking area, 500 meters away, and then drove her to the hospital.

ANALYSIS

The incident described is reminiscent of Lynn Hill's famous accident in Buoux, France, in which she fell at least 20 meters to the ground after failing to complete a figure 8 tie-in. This is clearly what happened in the accident described above. A properly and fully completed figure 8 will not suddenly untie or become detached. The climber likely began threading the rope end to retrace the initial figure 8 and then got sidetracked. As she pointed out, neither she nor her second checked her knot. In hindsight, the reporting climber acknowledged this was likely the case. Distraction may have been a factor, as well as fatigue or rushing because of the lateness of the day.

Always complete your tie-in without distraction, perform a check, and get your partner to inspect your knot before you climb. Also assess your belayer's readiness to belay.

It should be noted that the injured climber's partner left most of their gear in order to evacuate her partner. This was a good call. Unless the gear is required for rescue, first aid, evacuation, or safety, leave it behind. The rescuer's priority is the injured climber.

Editor's note: In late March, a ski mountaineer broke through a cornice during the famed Wapta Icefields traverse in the Canadian Rockies and survived a very long fall. The report about this accident and rescue can be found by searching "Balfour High Col" at publications.americanalpineclub.org.

STATISTICAL TABLES

TABLE I: REPORTED CLIMBING ACCIDENTS

Year	Number of Accidents Reported		Total Persons Involved		Injured		Fatalities	
	USA	CAN	USA	CAN	USA	CAN	USA	CAN
1951	15	n/a	22	n/a	11	n/a	3	n/a
1952	31	n/a	35	n/a	17	n/a	13	n/a
1953	24	n/a	27	n/a	12	n/a	12	n/a
1954	31	n/a	41	n/a	31	n/a	8	n/a
1955	34	n/a	39	n/a	28	n/a	6	n/a
1956	46	n/a	72	n/a	54	n/a	13	n/a
1957	45	n/a	53	n/a	28	n/a	18	n/a
1958	32	n/a	39	n/a	23	n/a	11	n/a
1959	42	2	56	2	31	0	19	2
1960	47	4	64	12	37	8	19	4
1961	49	9	61	14	45	10	14	4
1962	71	1	90	1	64	0	19	1
1963	68	11	79	12	47	10	19	2
1964	53	11	65	16	44	10	14	3
1965	72	0	90	0	59	0	21	0
1966	67	7	80	9	52	6	16	3
1967	74	10	110	14	63	7	33	5
1968	70	13	87	19	43	12	27	5
1969	94	11	125	17	66	9	29	2
1970	129	11	174	11	88	5	15	5
1971	110	17	138	29	76	11	31	7
1972	141	29	184	42	98	17	49	13
1973	108	6	131	6	85	4	36	2
1974	96	7	177	50	75	1	26	5
1975	78	7	158	22	66	8	19	2
1976	137	16	303	31	210	9	53	6
1977	121	30	277	49	106	21	32	11
1978	118	17	221	19	85	6	42	10
1979	100	36	137	54	83	17	40	19
1980	191	29	295	85	124	26	33	8
1981	97	43	223	119	80	39	39	6
1982	140	48	305	126	120	43	24	14
1983	187	29	442	76	169	26	37	7
1984	182	26	459	63	174	15	26	6
1985	195	27	403	62	190	22	17	3

Year	Number of Accidents Reported		Total Persons Involved		Injured		Fatalities	
	USA	CAN	USA	CAN	USA	CAN	USA	CAN
1986	203	31	406	80	182	25	37	14
1987	192	25	377	79	140	23	32	9
1988	156	18	288	44	155	18	24	4
1989	141	18	272	36	124	11	17	9
1990	136	25	245	50	125	24	24	4
1991	169	20	302	66	147	11	18	6
1992	175	17	351	45	144	11	43	6
1993	132	27	274	50	121	17	21	1
1994	158	25	335	58	131	25	27	5
1995	168	24	353	50	134	18	37	7
1996	139	28	261	59	100	16	31	6
1997	158	35	323	87	148	24	31	13
1998	138	24	281	55	138	18	20	1
1999	123	29	248	69	91	20	17	10
2000	150	23	301	36	121	23	24	7
2001	150	22	276	47	138	14	16	2
2002	139	27	295	29	105	23	34	6
2003	118	29	231	32	105	22	18	6
2004	160	35	311	30	140	16	35	14
2005	111	19	176	41	85	14	34	7
2006	109	n/a	227	n/a	89	n/a	21	n/a
2007	113	n/a	211	n/a	95	n/a	15	n/a
2008	112	n/a	203	n/a	96	n/a	19	n/a
2009	126	n/a	240	n/a	112	n/a	23	n/a
2010	185	n/a	389	n/a	151	n/a	34	n/a
2011	157	n/a	348	n/a	109	n/a	29	n/a
2012	140	15	309	36	121	12	30	2
2013	143	11	283	24	100	5	21	4
2014	112	10	170	19	89	8	28	1
2015	173	20	258	52	111	16	37	4
TOTAL:	7,481	1,014	13,806	2,134	6,231	756	1,630	303

TABLE II: ACCIDENTS BY LOCATION

Geographical Districts	1951–2014 Number of Accidents	Deaths	Total Persons Involved	2015 Number of Accidents	Deaths	Total Persons Involved
Canada*						
Alberta	545	145	1073	10	1	19
British Columbia	324	123	663	8	3	28
Yukon Territory	39	28	83	1	0	3
New Brunswick	1	0	0	0	0	0
Ontario	39	9	69	0	0	0
Quebec	31	10	63	1	0	2
East Arctic	8	2	21	0	0	0
West Arctic	2	2	2	0	0	0
United States						
Alaska	597	217	982	13	4	19
Arizona, Nevada, Texas	117	23	209	10	3	18
Atlantic–North	1119	156	1899	36	3	40
Atlantic–South	216	42	365	10	2	15
California	1494	315	850	26	6	35
Central	139	18	227	4	0	5
Colorado	934	240	2587	25	4	38
Montana, Idaho, South Dakota	98	40	155	2	1	4
Oregon	245	125	529	15	3	18
Utah, New Mex.	206	67	367	7	1	16
Washington	2025	336	1081	14	4	19
Wyoming	620	150	1139	11	6	31

*Canada figures include no data from 2006–2011; new data is included from 2012–2015

TABLE III: ACCIDENTS BY CAUSE

	1951–2014 USA	*1959–2014 CAN.	2015 USA	2015 CAN.
Terrain				
Rock	5120	550	114	13
Snow	2607	365	40	6
Ice	294	17	11	1
River	23	3	2	0
Unknown	22	11	0	0

	1951–2014 USA	*1959–2014 CAN.	2015 USA	2015 CAN.
Ascent or Descent				
Ascent	4132	603	72	12
Descent	1310	390	54	6
Unknown	268	13	14	0
Other[1]	26	0	5	2
Immediate Cause				
Fall or slip on rock	4042	298	56	9
Slip on snow or ice	1152	213	24	2
Falling rock, ice, or object	688	144	12	3
Exceeding abilities / Inexperience	590	36	13	0
Illness[2]	450	27	6	0
Stranded	392	60	12	2
Avalanche	327	128	4	2
Rappel Failure/Error[3]	382	53	16	1
Lowering Error	NA	NA	6	0
Exposure	282	14	3	0
Loss of control/glissade	231	18	9	0
Nut/cam pulled out	291	11	3	0
Failure to follow route	255	35	3	1
Fall into crevasse/moat	188	52	2	0
Faulty use of crampons	124	7	3	0
Piton/ice screw pulled out	95	13	0	0
Ascending too fast	74	0	1	0
Skiing[4]	70	14	0	0
Lightning	68	7	0	0
Equipment failure	17	3	1	0
Other[5]	621	38	4	1
Unknown	67	10	3	0
Contributory Causes				
Climbing unroped	1080	169	17	0
Exceeding abilities	1026	206	14	0
Placed no/inadequate protection	886	100	20	2
Inadequate equipment/clothing	748	73	13	0
Weather	537	73	3	3
Climbing alone	452	72	11	1
No helmet	381	73	9	2
Inadequate belay[6]	281	28	11	1
Nut/cam pulled out	225	32	8	0

	1951–2014 USA	*1959–2014 CAN.	2015 USA	2015 CAN.
Poor position	240	24	9	2
Darkness	177	21	7	1
Party separated	135	12	2	0
Failure to test holds	117	39	6	2
Piton/ice screw pulled out	86	14	1	0
Failed to follow directions	77	16	12	2
Exposure	67	16	1	0
Illness[2]	40	9	1	0
Equipment failure	19	7	1	0
Other[5]	308	100	16	2
Age of Individuals				
Under 15	1248	12	1	0
15-20	1336	204	10	0
21-25	1561	258	28	1
26-30	1470	211	40	3
31-35	2139	13	17	2
36-50	3495	143	27	1
Over 50	404	35	16	0
Unknown	2202	569	61	0
Sex[7]				
Male	NA	NA	131	21
Female	NA	NA	49	4
Not known	NA	NA	25	0
Experience Level				
None/Little	1918	308	13	0
Moderate (1 to 3 years)	1797	358	12	1
Experienced	2382	455	94	22
Unknown	2492	581	83	13
Month				
January	265	25	7	1
February	235	56	8	2
March	373	71	11	2
April	480	40	7	1
May	1021	65	15	1
June	1247	72	21	4
July	2089	266	16	1

August	1171	196	14	4
September	2053	76	16	1
October	514	42	8	0
November	237	20	8	2
December	129	24	5	0
Unknown	27	1	3	1
Type of Injury/Illness (Data since 1984)				
Fracture	1621	236	41	5
Laceration	832	76	16	5
Abrasion	411	79	6	0
Bruise	596	89	10	0
Sprain/strain	480	36	9	2
Concussion	333	30	12	1
Hypothermia	179	19	3	0
Frostbite	151	12	3	1
Dislocation	167	16	3	0
Puncture	55	14	0	0
Acute Mountain Sickness	50	0	1	0
HAPE	89	0	2	1
HACE	33	0	1	0
Other[8]	427	53	17	3
None	368	201	12	0

N.B. Data change: The 1986 and 1997 editions had some repeat data from previous years. The corrections are reflected in the cumulative data.

[1] Some accidents happen when climbers are at the top or bottom of a route, not climbing. They may be setting up a belay or rappel, or are just not anchored when they fall. This category was created in 2001. The category "unknown" is primarily because of solo climbers.

[2] These illnesses/injuries, which led directly or indirectly to an accident, included HAPE, HACE, and possible heart conditions.

[3] These included inadequate anchors, uneven ropes, no knots in rope ends, and inadequate anchor tethers. Prior years may have included lowering errors. "Lowering Error" was added as an independent category this year.

[4] This category covers ski mountaineering. Backcountry ski touring or snowshoeing incidents, including those involving avalanches, are not counted in these tables.

[5] These included failure to self-arrest, rope came unclipped from slings, cornice collapse, incorrect knot, rope cut by carabiner, inadequate tree anchor, no stopper knots, incomplete tie-in, and bear attack.

[6] These included miscommunication, ineffective belay, and no belay.

[7] This category is new this year. No prior data is available.

[8] These included spinal trauma, paralysis, head injuries, hair caught in rappel device, insect stings, bat bite, and bear bites.

Note: Injuries are counted only once in each category for a given incident. For example, an accident that results in three broken bones will only be listed once under "Fracture."

ACCIDENTS 1951-2014

WHERE

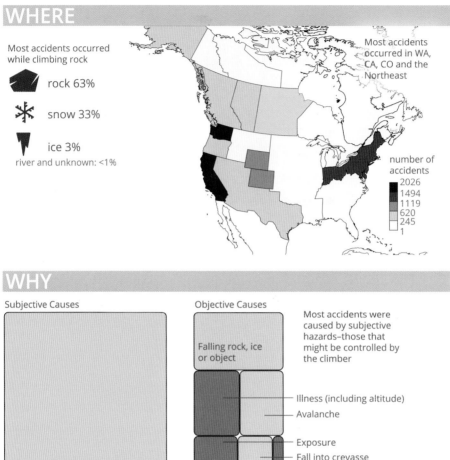

Most accidents occurred while climbing rock

rock 63%

snow 33%

ice 3%

river and unknown: <1%

Most accidents occurred in WA, CA, CO and the Northeast

number of accidents
2026
1494
1119
620
245
1

WHY

Subjective Causes

fall or slip on rock

slip on snow or ice

exceeding abilities

○ climber action
● equipment

Objective Causes

Falling rock, ice or object

Illness (including altitude)
Avalanche
Exposure
Fall into crevasse
Lightning

○ terrain
● elements

stranded
rappel error
nut pulled out
off route
loss control/glissade
faulty use of crampons
piton/screw pulled out
skiing
ascending too fast
equipment failure

Most accidents were caused by subjective hazards–those that might be controlled by the climber

WHEN

ascent 70%

descent 25%

unknown and other: 5%

moderate

experienced

Climbers of all experience levels were involved

Design: MichaelSkaug.com